Language Remediation and Expansion

100 SKILL-BUILDING REFERENCE LISTS

by Catharine S. Bush, M.A.
Speech-Language Pathologist, CCC

Illustrated by
Don Bush

Communication Skill Builders, Inc.
3130 N. Dodge Blvd./P.O. Box 42050
Tucson, Arizona 85733

LB
1576
B94

ISBN 0-88450-797-1
Catalog No. 3052

INTRODUCTION

This handbook has been designed as a source book for the remediation of language learning problems, for language skill development, and for expansion and enrichment of language. The 100 lists can be used in many ways by the creative and resourceful specialist or teacher. Suggested activities that emphasize *communicative interaction* and *experience-based* language precede each list. Acting-out language and verbalizing words and ideas in meaningful contexts encourage the retention of the content and facilitate learning of individual skills.

Because most of the skills lists are sequenced in order of difficulty, the specialist or teacher may begin at the appropriate level for the individual student or group after needs have been determined, and continue through the exercises until the desired goal has been attained. Objectives have been provided for each list which may be helpful in preparing individualized education plans (IEP). Interesting and relevant material in the 1-8 grade range has been selected in order that students will enjoy the learning of language.

Creative responses are encouraged. Many of the items allow multiple responses so each student answer should be carefully considered. More items may be added to the lists as they are used.

The book is divided into five main sections with extensive skill-building or reference lists in each:

1. Sounds of Language (phonology)
2. Structure of Language (morphology and syntax)
3. Meaning of Language (semantics and comprehension)
4. Thinking with Language (cognitive tasks)
5. Production of Language (non-verbal, verbal and written)

The lists are cross referenced to provide related activities to reinforce and extend the skills being taught. Ideas are also presented for making learning materials for extended practice in class and/or at home.

The activities may be used with individual students or groups and many may be utilized with whole classes. The materials have been compiled and developed from the author's experience as a classroom teacher and Speech-Language Pathologist. They have also been used successfully in the following applications:

carryover activities in articulation modification
voice and fluency training
hearing impaired programs
bilingual programs
language development programs.

It is hoped that this volume will provide an efficient way for specialists and teachers to make language learning meaningful, lively, enjoyable, and above all, functional for their students.

My deepest appreciation goes to Teresa Banks, Speech-Language Pathologist, who provided many valuable ideas for this book and spent hours proofreading. Special thanks go to Kevin, Daniel and Michele Bush for their useful ideas and suggestions.

Catharine S. Bush

The use of the masculine pronoun form throughout the book is for convenience and brevity and is not intended to be preferential or discriminatory.

Contents

I. **Sounds of Language (phonology)** 1

    List 1:   Phonograms. 3

    List 2:   Rhyming Sentences. 6

    Lists 3-6:   Syllabication. 8

        List 3:   1-Syllable Words. 8

        List 4:   2-Syllable Words. 9

        List 5:   3-Syllable Words. 9

        List 6:   4-, 5- and 6-Syllable Words 10

    Lists 7-10: Sound Blending. 11

        List 7:   2-Phoneme Words. 11

        List 8:   3-Phoneme Words. 12

        List 9:   4-Phoneme Words. 12

        List 10: 5-Phoneme Words. 13

II. **Structure of Language (morphology and syntax)** 15

    List 11:   Irregular Verbs. 17

    List 12:   Irregular Plurals. 20

    Lists 13-14: Prefixes and Suffixes. 21

        List 13: Prefixes. 21

        List 14: Suffixes. 22

    Lists 15-16: Scrambled Sentences. 24

        List 15: Scrambled 3-Word Sentences 24

        List 16: Scrambled 4-Word Sentences 26

    List 17:   Constructing Sentences 27

    List 18:   Contractions 28

III. **Meaning of Language (semantics and comprehension)**. 29

    Lists 19-20: Basic Concepts 31

        List 19: Basic Concepts 31

        List 20: Basic Concept Activities 33

    Lists 21-22: Compound Words 37

        List 21: Compound Words 37

        List 22: Compound Word Activities 40

    Lists 23-25: Homophones. 41

        List 23: Level I. 41

        List 24: Level II 45

        List 25: Level III 49

    List 26:   Homographs 53

    List 27:   Heteronyms. 61

Lists 28–30: Antonyms 63
    List 28: Level I 63
    List 29: Level II 64
    List 30: Level III 65

List 31:   Adjectives 66

Lists 32–33: Adverbs 69
    List 32: Adverbs 69
    List 33: Acting Adverbs 70

List 34:   Abbreviations 71

List 35:   Similes 73

Lists 36–39: Idioms 74
    List 36: Food and Colors 74
    List 37: Animals 75
    List 38: Parts of Body 75
    List 39: Other 77

List 40:   Proverbs 80

Lists 41–42: Scrambled Sentence Sequence 82
    List 41: 2–Sentence Sequence .82
    List 42: 3–Sentence Sequence .84

Lists 43–46: Incomplete Sentences 87
    List 43: Level I 87
    List 44: Level II 88
    List 45: Level III 89
    List 46: Level IV 90

Lists 47–49: Following Directions 92
    List 47: Following 2 Directions 92
    List 48: Following 3 Directions 94
    List 49: Giving and Following Directions 95

Lists 50–51: Synonyms 96
    List 50: Rhyming Synonyms 96
    List 51: 2–Syllable Rhyming Synonyms 98

IV. Thinking with Language 99

Lists 52–62: Analogies 101
    List 52: Characteristics 101
    List 53: Part/Whole 103
    List 54: Whole/Part 104
    List 55: Location 105
    List 56: Action/Object 106
    List 57: Agent — Action or Object 107
    List 58: Class or Synonym 108
    List 59: Familial 109
    List 60: Grammatical 110
    List 61: Temporal/Sequential 111
    List 62: Antonyms 112

Lists 63–64: Categories 113
    List 63: Level I 113
    List 64: Level II 115

Lists 65–68: Classification 117
    List 65: Level I 117
    List 66: Level II 119

List 67:   Level III 120
List 68:   Level IV 121

Lists 69–70: Part-Whole Relationships 122
    List 69:   Level I 122
    List 70:   Level II 124

Lists 71–73: Associations 125
    List 71:   Level I 125
    List 72:   Level II 127
    List 73:   Level III 128

Lists 74–75: Similarities/Differences 129
    List 74:   Level I 129
    List 75:   Level II 130

Lists 76–77: Absurd Sentences 131
    List 76:   Absurd Sentences 131
    List 77:   Absurd Sentences with Rhyming Words 133

Lists 78–79: Inferences (riddles) 135
    List 78:   Level I 135
    List 79:   Level II 139

List 80:   Logical Sequences 142

V. Production of Language (non-verbal, verbal, written) 145

    List 81:   Body Language, Beginning Level 147
    List 82:   Body Language, Advanced — Sports 149
    List 83:   Body Language, Advanced — Occupations 152
    List 84:   Body Language, Advanced — Emotions and Feelings 156
    List 85:   Body Language, Advanced — Transportation ...157
    List 86:   Body Language, Advanced — Locations 158
    List 87:   Sequence of Actions 160
    List 88:   Production of Sentences 162
    List 89:   Descriptive Language 165
    List 90:   Story-Telling 166

    Lists 91–92: Demonstration Talks and Mini-Talks 168
        List 91:   Demonstration Talks 168
        List 92:   Mini-Talks 170

    List 93:   People Talks 171
    List 94:   Commercials and Announcements 173
    List 95:   Interview Topics 175
    List 96:   Improvisations 177

VI. Helpful Lists 179

    List 97:   Famous People 181
    List 98:   Historical Events 182
    List 99:   Fictional Characters 184
    List 100:   Other Stories for Improvisation 186

Appendix 189

Skills Index 205

I. Sounds of Language (phonology)

1. Phonograms — rhyming words
2. Rhyming sentences
3. Syllabication, 1-syllable words
4. Syllabication, 2-syllable words
5. Syllabication, 3-syllable words
6. Syllabication, 4-, 5-, 6-syllable words
7. Sound blending, 2-phoneme words
8. Sound blending, 3-phoneme words
9. Sound blending, 4-phoneme words
10. Sound blending, 5-phoneme words

List 1: Phonograms

OBJECTIVE

To develop the student's ability to discriminate likenesses and differences heard in words, and understand and use the words in correct context.

APPLICATIONS

- Present a series of words orally, including several from one phonogram group and one from another group. Student should recognize the word that does not rhyme. Explain the meanings of unfamiliar words to expand vocabularies.

- Give the student a list of phonogram groups. Student can make sentences using rhyming pairs and illustrate them in a "Have You Seen" book. See illustration.

- Print rhyming pairs on cards. One or two students pantomime the words on the card consecutively. Other students guess what the words are. Remind them that the words sound alike.

ab	cab, dab, gab, jab, tab, crab, drab, grab, flab, slab, scab, stab	**alk**	talk, walk, chalk, stalk
ace	face, lace, mace, pace, brace, grace, trace, place, space	**all**	ball, call, fall, gall, hall, mall, pall, tall, wall, small, stall
ack	back, hack, jack, lack, pack, rack, sack, tack, black, clack, slack, crack, shack, smack, snack, knack, quack, track	**am**	bam, dam, ham, jam, ram, tam, clam, slam, cram, dram, tram, wham, sham
ad	bad, cad, fad, dad, had, lad, mad, pad, sad, tad, glad, brad, clad	**ame**	came, dame, fame, game, lame, name, same, tame, blame, flame, frame, shame
ade	fade, made, jade, wade, blade, grade, shade, trade, spade, glade	**amp**	damp, lamp, ramp, champ, clamp, cramp, tramp, stamp
ag	bag, gag, hag, jag, lag, nag, sag, tag, rag, wag, brag, drag, crag, snag, stag, flag, shag	**an**	ban, can, fan, man, pan, ran, tan, van, scan
age	cage, page, rage, sage, wage, stage	**ane**	bane, lane, mane, pane, sane, vane, wane, crane, plane
aid	laid, paid, maid, raid, braid, afraid	**ank**	bank, rank, sank, tank, crank, clank, blank, thank, spank, plank
ail	bail, fail, hail, jail, mail, nail, pail, rail, sail, tail, wail, frail, trail, flail, snail, quail	**are**	bare, dare, fare, mare, pare, rare, blare, spare, flare, glare, scare, snare, stare, share
ain	gain, lain, main, rain, brain, drain, grain, chain, train, slain, strain, stain	**at**	bat, cat, fat, hat, mat, pat, rat, vat, gnat, that, spat, flat, chat
aint	faint, paint, saint, quaint	**ate**	date, fate, gate, hate, late, mate, rate, crate, grate, state, slate
air	fair, hair, pair, chair, stair	**ead**	dead, head, lead, read, bread, dread, tread
ake	bake, cake, fake, lake, make, rake, sake, take, wake, flake, snake, stake, brake, shake	**eat**	beat, feat, heat, meat, neat, seat, cheat, bleat, treat
ale	bale, dale, gale, male, pale, tale, scale, stale, whale	**eck**	deck, neck, peck, speck, check, wreck

3

Phonograms (continued)

ed   bed, fed, led, red, wed, fled, bled, sled, bred, sped

eed   deed, feed, heed, need, reed, seed, weed, bleed, creed, greed, breed, speed, tweed

eek   meek, peek, seek, week, creek, sleek, cheek

eel   feel, heel, peel, reel, kneel, steel, wheel

eep   deep, keep, peep, seep, weep, creep, sleep, steep, sweep, sheep

ear   fear, dear, gear, hear, near, rear, sear, tear, clear, smear, spear

eer   beer, deer, leer, peer, veer, sneer, steer, cheer, sheer

eet   beet, feet, meet, greet, sheet, sleet, sweet, fleet, tweet

eeze   breeze, freeze, sneeze, squeeze, wheeze

ell   bell, cell, dell, fell, sell, shell, smell, spell, swell

en   den, hen, men, pen, ten, then, when, wren

end   bend, lend, mend, send, tend, blend, spend, trend

ent   bent, cent, dent, gent, lent, sent, tent, vent, went, spent

ess   less, mess, bless, chess, dress, press, stress

est   best, jest, nest, pest, test, vest, west, blest, chest

ew   few, dew, new, pew, flew, knew, chew, grew, stew, brew

ice   dice, lice, mice, nice, rice, vice, price, slice, spice, twice

ick   hick, lick, nick, pick, sick, tick, wick, quick, flick, click, slick, brick, trick, chick, stick, thick

id   bid, did, hid, kid, rid, grid, skid, slid, squid

ide   bide, hide, ride, side, tide, glide, slide, pride

ight   fight, light, might, night, right, sight, tight, bright, fright, flight, knight

ike   bike, dike, hike, like, mike, pike, spike, strike

ile   file, mile, pile, tile, smile, stile, while

ill   bill, dill, fill, gill, hill, kill, mill, pill, sill, will, chill, drill, grill, trill, frill, thrill, skill, spill, still

ime   dime, lime, mime, time, chime, crime, grime, prime

in   bin, din, fin, gin, kin, pin, sin, tin, win, chin, grin, skin, spin, thin, twin

ind   kind, mind, find, bind, wind, rind, blind, grind

ine   dine, fine, mine, pine, vine, wine, shine, spine, brine, thine, twine

ing   ding, king, ring, sing, wing, bring, spring, cling, sling, sting, swing, string, thing

ink   kink, link, mink, rink, sink, wink, pink, blink, drink, stink, think, shrink

int   hint, lint, mint, tint, flint, glint, sprint, squint, stint, print

ip   dip, hip, nip, rip, sip, tip, chip, clip, flip, drip, grip, trip, skip, snip, slip, ship, whip

ipe   pipe, ripe, wipe, snipe, gripe, swipe, stripe

ire   fire, dire, hire, mire, sire, tire, wire, spire

irt   dirt, flirt, skirt, shirt, squirt

it   bit, fit, hit, kit, lit, pit, sit, wit, grit, knit, quit, slit, flit

ite   bite, mite, rite, site, quite, spite, write, sprite

ive   five, dive, hive, live, chive, strive, thrive, drive

oat   boat, coat, goat, moat, float, gloat, throat, bloat

ock   dock, hock, lock, mock, sock, tock, rock, block, flock, crock, knock, shock, stock

oil   boil, coil, foil, soil, toil, broil, spoil

oke   coke, joke, poke, woke, broke, choke, smoke, stroke, stoke, spoke

old   bold, cold, fold, gold, hold, mold, sold, told, scold

ole   dole, hole, mole, pole, sole, stole, whole

one   bone, cone, lone, tone, shone, throne, alone, prone, drone, crone

ong   dong, gong, long, song, thong, prong, wrong, strong, throng

ook   book, cook, hook, look, nook, rook, took, brook, crook, shook

ool   cool, fool, pool, tool, drool, spool, stool, school

oom	boom, doom, loom, room, gloom, broom, groom	**ub**	dub, cub, hub, pub, rub, sub, tub, club, grub, stub, scrub, shrub
oop	hoop, loop, droop, scoop, swoop, troop, stoop	**uck**	buck, duck, luck, muck, puck, suck, tuck, chuck, cluck, stuck, truck
op	cop, hop, mop, pop, top, chop, crop, drop, prop, shop, stop	**udge**	budge, fudge, judge, nudge, grudge, smudge, trudge
ore	bore, core, fore, more, sore, tore, wore, shore, snore, store	**ug**	bug, dug, hug, jug, lug, mug, pug, tug, rug, drug, plug, snug, smug
ose	hose, nose, pose, rose, chose, close, those	**um**	bum, hum, gum, rum, sum, drum, plum, slum, scum, chum
oss	boss, loss, moss, toss, cross, gloss	**ump**	bump, dump, hump, jump, lump, pump, rump, plump, stump, clump, thump, grump, trump
ot	cot, got, hot, lot, pot, tot, rot, blot, knot, plot, trot, shot		
ote	note, rote, tote, vote, quote	**un**	bun, fun, gun, nun, pun, run, sun, spun, stun
ought	bought, fought, thought, brought, sought	**unch**	bunch, lunch, munch, punch, brunch, crunch, hunch
ound	bound, found, hound, mound, round, pound, sound, wound, ground	**ung**	hung, lung, rung, sung, clung, swung, sprung, stung
out	bout, gout, pout, rout, scout, spout, stout, snout, shout, trout	**unk**	bunk, dunk, hunk, junk, punk, sunk, chunk, drunk, skunk, flunk, plunk, trunk
ōw	bow, low, mow, row, sow, tow, crow, blow, glow, know, show	**unt**	bunt, hunt, punt, runt, grunt, blunt, stunt, shunt
ow	bow, cow, how, now, pow, sow, vow, wow, brow, plow, chow	**ush**	hush, mush, lush, rush, gush, blush, crush, thrush, flush, plush
owl	fowl, howl, jowl, growl, prowl	**ust**	bust, dust, just, must, rust, crust, trust
own	down, gown, town, brown, drown, frown, clown	**ut**	cut, gut, hut, nut, rut, glut, shut, strut

List 2: Rhyming Sentences

Buffalo Bill took a pill.

OBJECTIVE

To develop the student's ability to supply appropriate rhyming words in sentences based on context clues and sound similarities perceived.

APPLICATIONS

+ Read the sentence emphasizing the first underlined word and omitting the last word. The student should fill in the rhyming word. Then reinforce by saying the two words together: "small, Paul." Accept other appropriate words that rhyme.

+ Have students make up their own rhyming sentences using List 1, Phonograms.

Students can make up sentences using List 97, Famous People, and List 99, Fictional Characters.

Try these out on other students or families.

example: Buffalo <u>Bill</u> took a <u>pill.</u>
Snow <u>White</u> had a <u>fight.</u>

+ Refer to List 43, Incomplete Sentences, for a similar sentence completion activity, Also see List 77, Absurd Sentences.

1. The little <u>mouse</u> went in the ___house___ .
2. Little <u>Mike</u> rode his ___bike___ .
3. My old <u>shirt</u> is covered with ___dirt___ .
4. My <u>dad</u> was very ___mad___ .
5. Sue will <u>bake</u> a chocolate ___cake___ .
6. We had <u>fun</u> in the hot ___sun___ .
7. The man in <u>jail</u> got some ___mail___ .
8. The golf <u>ball</u> is very ___small___ .
9. The hot old <u>man</u> turned on the ___fan___ .
10. Put the <u>jar</u> in the ___car___ .
11. Please don't <u>waste</u> the jar of ___paste___ .
12. The black <u>bat</u> flew over the ___cat___ .
13. The funny <u>seal</u> ate his ___meal___ .
14. The bad <u>dream</u> made me ___scream___ .
15. You need <u>heat</u> to cook the ___meat___ .
16. I fell out of <u>bed</u> and hurt my ___head___ .
17. The Boy Scout <u>went</u> into his ___tent___ .
18. I can <u>guess</u> who made this ___mess___ .
19. The bird will <u>rest</u> in his ___nest___ .
20. Little <u>Sue</u> said, "I know ___you___ ."
21. The little <u>chick</u> sat on a ___stick___ .
22. The naughty <u>kid</u> ran and ___hid___ .
23. We will <u>hide</u> under the ___slide___ .
24. The new flash<u>light</u> was very ___bright___ .
25. My brother <u>Mike</u> loves to ___hike___ .
26. Poor sick <u>Bill</u> took a ___pill___ .
27. Juan bought a <u>lime</u> for just a ___dime___ .
28. Do you <u>like</u> to ride your ___bike___ ?
29. Billy's <u>twin</u> is very ___thin___ .
30. The bees can <u>dive</u> into the ___hive___ .
31. The lemonade is <u>pink</u> and good to <u>drink</u> .
32. The sailor left his <u>coat</u> on the sail<u>boat</u>.
33. Uncle <u>Paul</u> bounced a ___ball___ .
34. The king sat <u>alone</u> on his ___throne___ .

35. The old crook stole a _____ book _____ .
36. The coffee pot was very _____ hot _____ .
37. My father found a weed on the ground .
38. The circus clown wears the color brown .
39. Did you scrub that dirty _____ tub _____ ?
40. The little duck had bad _____ luck _____ .
41. Lucy dropped her mug on the new rug .
42. The old bum played his _____ drum _____ .
43. Jack Horner got a plum on his thumb .
44. Henry caught a bug in his _____ jug _____ .
45. Never run holding a _____ gun _____ .
46. We found a skunk in a pile of junk .
47. The big black bear broke his chair .
48. I left the boat's oar on the _____ shore _____ .
49. Will you look at my new _____ book _____ ?
50. At our school we have a swimming pool .
51. That silly song was much too _____ long _____ .
52. I felt a rock in my _____ sock _____ .
53. I got my hair caught in the _____ chair _____ .
54. My puppy chews my dad's old shoes .
55. It's not funny to lose your _____ money _____ .
56. I was wishing I could go _____ fishing _____ .
57. I hurt my heel on the car's _____ wheel _____ .
58. Put your feet under the _____ sheet _____ .
59. If you stand in the breeze, it will make you _____ sneeze _____ .
60. The bird flew into my _____ shoe _____ .
61. How much is the price of that pair of _____ dice _____ ?
62. The sailor did a flip on the big _____ ship _____ .
63. Wrap the wire around the _____ tire _____ .
64. The traffic cop cleaned the floor with a _____ mop _____ .
65. I mixed some spice into the _____ rice _____ .
66. Bob told a joke and drank a _____ coke _____ .
67. I made some jello that turned out yellow .
68. There's a full moon in the month of June.

69. I get a shiver when I swim in the _____ river _____ .
70. Do you remember the month before December?
71. Draw a heart on the _____ chart _____ .
72. Don't lay the poster on the _____ toaster _____ .
73. I'll sell you this rhyme for just a _____ dime _____ .
74. I put the fish on the green _____ dish _____ .
75. I saw a horse on the golf _____ course _____ .
76. I eat tomatoes and big brown potatoes .
77. The little billy goat went sailing in a boat.
78. Hold the chair up in the _____ air _____ .
79. I saw a frog sitting on a _____ log _____ .
80. Pour the ink down the _____ sink _____ .
81. Listen to me talk, then write with the _____ chalk _____ .
82. Open the door, then sit on the _____ floor _____ .
83. After the dog is fed, pat him on the head.
84. In school you play; in church you pray .
85. The pretty nurse carried a _____ purse _____ .
86. The soup was so thick, it made me sick .
87. The little gray moth ate all the _____ cloth _____ .
88. In libraries there are books; in kitchens there are _____ cooks _____ .
89. The little yellow duck rode in the truck .
90. The cold little kittens put on their _____ mittens.
91. Catch the fox and put it in the _____ box _____ .
92. We bought a bunny with our _____ money _____ .
93. You left your skate down by the _____ gate _____ .
94. We stood in the rain waiting for the train.
95. The dog dropped his bone when he heard the _____ phone _____ .
96. I went to sleep and dreamed about sheep.
97. The old raccoon ate his soup with a spoon.
98. Jan found a green snake in the blue lake.
99. Lucy threw the ball against the red wall .
100. The chef will bake a chocolate _____ cake _____ .

Lists 3–6: Syllabication

OBJECTIVE

To develop the student's ability to identify word parts as an aid to sequencing syllables into meaningful words.

APPLICATIONS

♦ Present words from Lists 3 and 4 verbally. Students should tell whether words have one or two syllables. Then use Lists 5 and 6 in the same activity as the student succeeds at each level. Have the students use some of the words in sentences or tell the meanings.

♦ Clap out or beat out syllables as they are said orally.

♦ Show the students small objects or toys. They should determine the number of syllables in the names.

♦ For oral-motor coordination practice, have the student repeat after you the 4-, 5-, and 6-syllable words. Use them in sentences also. Words the student is having difficulty with can be printed on flash cards and sent home for additional practice.

List 3: 1-Syllable Words

pet	scream	pig	splash	buzz
squirm	squeak	bounce	toes	cloud
bat	ghost	fangs	church	boom
blood	zoo	cake	crash	sweet
fly	king	ski	egg	prize
golf	gift	frog	flip	June
snake	kite	watch	school	Mars
bell	hush	fierce	moon	space
cry	kick	bow	park	bug
ball	rose	dad	gold	dream
hear	bright	bath	swamp	tube
ice	chips	pop	flame	hike
trash	wings	rich	fast	swim
win	game	play	stage	eat
pie	trick	treat	May	cute
doll	spring	clothes	gross	cool
scare	cat	witch	toad	worm
kind	queen	prince	ace	test
game	lose	truck	cards	chess
sun	moon	stars	ship	rocks
wish	red	blue	green	orange
weird	strange	dime	March	mom

List 4: 2-Syllable Words

wiggle	aardvark	banjo	treasure	mongoose
gallop	walrus	monster	lagoon	creature
lightning	scary	Christmas	present	haunted
creepy	crackle	tiger	Batman	peanuts
Snoopy	spider	bunny	kitty	swimming
candy	pickle	dessert	balloon	whisper
model	ballet	princess	tennis	hockey
camping	rescue	summer	police	giant
robot	recess	winter	athlete	bacon
music	cyclone	trophy	quarter	bowling
beetle	marbles	bubble	kitten	finger
pumpkin	villain	hero	giraffe	crazy
tomcat	movies	party	happy	mistake
dimple	tummy	phantom	doctor	cartoon
shadow	jungle	panther	parade	juggler
disguise	costume	Easter	riddle	porpoise
ocean	contest	winner	polite	sandal
deckers	mountain	chairman	mother	raisins
thunder	teacher	apples	popcorn	diving
comics	Lucy	evil	soda	crossroad
barnyard	blowout	carefree	cowpoke	downstream
earring	fairground	hallway	handcuff	mainland
newsstand	guitar	zebra	stapler	sawmill
scarecrow	seaport	foreword	snowplow	sparerib
surfboard	teaspoon	trademark	uproot	weekend

List 5: 3-Syllable Words

roadrunner	elephant	chimpanzee	kangaroo
Dracula	Frankenstein	Halloween	Superman
photograph	Spiderman	Thanksgiving	popsicle
dangerous	allowance	basketball	vacation
gymnastics	daffodil	exciting	fantastic
musketeer	telephone	glittering	bicycle
mystery	troublesome	lunatic	strawberry
astronaut	mosquito	victory	telescope
dinosaur	Washington	umbrella	barbeque
theater	potato	hamburger	remember
banana	ambulance	disgusting	enchanted
somersault	October	December	Saturday
typewriter	principal	horrible	janitor
library	donation	equator	happily
cantaloupe	spaghetti	tornado	tomato
November	tricycle	gorilla	telegram
procession	prescription	instruction	delightful
carnival	skyscraper	camera	carpenter
unpleasant	autograph	atmosphere	cucumber
excellent	moccasin	patio	screwdriver
volcano	collection	humorous	pajamas

List 6: 4-, 5- and 6-Syllable Words

4-Syllable Words

rhinoceros	orangutang	adventurous	thermometer
inheritance	alligator	helicopter	aluminum
embarrassment	military	constitution	kaleidoscope
melodrama	nobility	Arizona	vaccination
revolution	television	ridiculous	environment
January	secretary	remarkable	dictionary
coincidence	accidental	aquarium	superstitious
material	escalator	elevator	Italian
American	Mississippi	mechanical	celebration
calculator	entertainment	disappointed	education
electrical	advertisement	fashionable	intelligent
caterpillar	ornamental	kindergarten	binoculars
biology	recreation	emergency	substitution
preposition	irregular	Cinderella	Pinocchio
Rumpelstiltskin	motorcycle	sentimental	regulation
insulation	generator	microscopic	February
inventory	transportation	subdivision	psychologist
patriotic	automatic	majority	appreciate
altogether	evaporate	arithmetic	independence
literature	energetic	rectangular	photographer
scientific	cemetery	astronomer	impractical

5-Syllable Words

California	executioner	indispensable	astronomical
antibiotic	representative	disagreeable	supplementary
extraordinary	congratulations	international	Louisiana
exaggeration	chronological	individual	refrigerator
anniversary	pediatrician	precipitation	recommendation
multiplication	transcontinental	coordination	intermediate
association	elementary		

6-Syllable Words

encyclopedia	veterinarian

Lists 7–10: Sound Blending

OBJECTIVE

To develop the student's ability to synthesize sounds heard into meaningful words.

APPLICATIONS

- Present the words orally, pausing one-half second between phonemes, starting with List 8. Use the words in sentences first and later as isolated words. The student tells you the word.

    example: The boy hurt his th — igh.

    Proceed to succeeding lists as he masters each list. Repeat the word if necessary.

- Tell the students you will only use words from one category such as parts of the body, things in the room, or sports. Refer to Lists 82 through 86 to select other words.

    After the student has blended the word, have him tell you something about it in a sentence.

    example: c—r—a—sh. "Crash — Our car got in a crash."

- For a discrimination activity, ask the student to tell what consonant sound he hears at the beginning or end of the word. Choose appropriate words from the lists.

List 7: 2-Phoneme Words

sh — oe	k — ey	t — ea	sh — e
M — ay	ou — ch	t — ie	a — ll
kn — ee	n — o	s — ee	p — ay
i — tch	ch — ew	b — oo	h — ay
m — e	th — igh	p — ie	l — ay
h — igh	th — ough	a — che	g — o
c — ow	r — ow	e — gg	s — ay
ea — t	r — ay	a — pe	l — ow
b — oy	i — f	a — ce	m — ow
b — ee	a — sh	a — te	t — oe
t — oo	a — ge	ee — l	l — aw
s — o	J — oe	u — p	a — m
d — oe	ou — t	u — s	a — t
m — oo	t — oy	s — ee	ea — ch
o — dd	b — uy	sh — ow	sh — y
o — ff	g — uy	n — ew	j — aw
z — oo	l — ie	m — y	h — oe
b — ow	a — dd	i — s	s — igh
d — ay	d — ie	s — ue	

11

List 8: 3-Phoneme Words

ch — ee — k	g — u — n	k — i — ck	b — a — th
c — oo — l	b — ur — n	h — o — t	p — ea — ch
m — a — tch	a — pp — le	p — u — p	r — ea — d
t — ee — th	wr — e — ck	c — a — t	z — i — p
l — a — mb	c — u — b	h — o — me	t — oe — s
p — ur — se	p — oo — l	f — oo — t	s — i — ght
m — a — th	s — i — ck	l — e — g	g — oa — t
ch — ea — t	t — i — re	n — e — ck	r — o — pe
b — ir — d	s — ur — f	h — ea — d	p — i — g
w — i — sh	c — a — ke	sh — ee — p	h — o — g
s — u — n	s — ea — l	ch — i — n	t — oa — d
l — i — p	s — oa — p	th — u — mb	th — i — n
b — a — d	ch — a — lk	n — a — il	l — i — ght
n — o — se	ch — e — ck	c — oa — t	th — i — ck
s — i — ng	f — oo — l	d — o — g	g — a — me
n — i — ght	m — a — p	c — o — t	a — n — t
w — a — tch	g — a — me	s — a — d	sh — e — d
f — i — re	t — a — pe	k — i — t	h — ou — se
m — ou — se	n — a — me	r — ai — n	b — o — wl
sh — ir — t	w — i — th	s — ai — l	k — i — d
d — u — ck	r — e — d	wr — e — ck	j — o — g
d — i — me	m — oo — n	t — i — me	m — i — ght
b — e — d	t — a — ck	l — ear — n	t — i — ck
k — i — te	t — a — il	r — i — ch	
w — i — n	f — u — n		

List 9: 4-Phoneme Words

p — o — n — y	b — o — d — y	c — a — m — p	p — i — g — s
c — oo — k — ie	g — o — l — d	gh — o — s — t	m — e — n — u
f — i — ng — er	p — ur — p — le	w — a — t — er	ch — e — s — t
k — i — ss — ed	w — or — l — d	b — a — b — y	c — o — l — d
wr — i — s — t	n — ee — d — le	p — a — p — er	f — o — l — d
t — ur — t — le	s — o — f — t	h — a — pp — y	j — o — ck — ey
g — ir — a — ffe	s — a — dd — le	p — ai — n — t	l — a — d — y
k — i — tt — en	k — i — tch — en	b — u — nn — y	m — i — tt — en
s — u — mm — er	t — ur — k — ey	f — a — th — er	s — o — l — d
p — e — nn — y	f — a — s — t	ch — i — l — d	c — ur — l — s
n — i — ck — el	r — a — n — ch	r — u — l — er	kn — u — ck — le
h — o — ck — ey	d — a — n — ce	p — i — ck — le	a — n — k — le
s — o — cc — er	f — u — nn — y	p — u — n — t	t — u — mm — y
m — o — v — ie	t — a — tt — oo	m — i — l — k	s — i — ng — er
b — u — bb — le	l — u — n — ch	p — i — ll — ow	l — a — m — p
t — ea — ch — er	m — o — th — er	d — u — ck — s	f — ai — n — t

12

List 10: 5-Phoneme Words

b – ir – th – d – ay	birthday	p – o – s – t – er	poster
r – o – d – e – o	rodeo	m – a – g – i – c	magic
m – o – n – k – ey	monkey	c – ir – c – u – s	circus
c – a – m – p – er	camper	c – ou – s – i – n	cousin
t – e – nn – i – s	tennis	s – ur – f – i – ng	surfing
p – o – l – i – ce	police	p – ea – c – o – ck	peacock
r – a – bb – i – t	rabbit	p – u – pp – e – t	puppet
g – oo – d – b – y	goodby	j – a – ck – et	jacket
s – ai – l – i – ng	sailing	sh – ou – l – d – er	shoulder
s – i – s – t – er	sister	w – i – n – d – ow	window
l – e – tt – er – s	letters	M – o – n – d – ay	Monday
p – ai – n – t – er	painter	m – u – s – i – c	music
S – u – n – d – ay	Sunday	p – e – n – c – il	pencil
c – a – m – er – a	camera	e – r – a – s – er	eraser
c – oo – k – ie – s	cookies	A – p – r – i – l	April
d – o – c – t – or	doctor	T – ue – s – d – ay	Tuesday
t – oa – s – t – er	toaster		

II. Structure of Language
(morphology and syntax)

Mouse, mice; moose ... MEECE?

11. Irregular verbs

12. Irregular plurals

13. Prefixes

14. Suffixes

15. Scrambled 3-word sentences

16. Scrambled 4-word sentences

17. Constructing sentences (declarative, interrogative, exclamatory)

18. Contractions

List 11: Irregular Verbs

OBJECTIVE

To develop the student's ability to identify and use the correct forms of common irregular verbs in functional language.

APPLICATIONS

◆ Teach similar irregular verbs as a group; e.g.,

verbs that remain the same   (bet — bet — has bet)
                                             (cut — cut — has cut)

verbs that have the same form for past and past participle   (hear — heard — has heard)
                                             (say — said — has said)

verbs that use the root word in the past participle but change for past tense (fall — fell — has fallen)
                                             (forgive — forgave — has forgiven)

Bit

Bite

Has bitten

◆ To practice the verb form, keep the verb constant and change the subject.

Example: The boy hit the dog.
              Snoopy hit the dog.
              The baby hit the dog.
              The cat hit the dog.

Use pictures to represent the subject and/or the direct object.

◆ Keep the subject constant and show pictures of the actions.

Example: Mary has slept in the chair.
              Mary has read the book.
              Mary has played the game.

◆ Say a sentence using the present form of the verb and perform the action with small objects. "The boy is catching the dog." Then ask, "What did he just do?" to elicit the past tense. "The boy caught the dog."

◆ Have the student tell mini-fairy tales to practice syntactic carryover. Refer to Lists 99 and 100. Tell a simple version of the story first to the student using the desired constructions.

Present	Past	Past Participle
am	was	been
are (pl.)	were	been
beat	beat	beaten
begin	began	begun
bend	bent or bended	bent or bended
bet	bet	bet
bite	bit	bitten
bleed	bled	bled
blow	blew	blown
break	broke	broken
bring	brought	brought
build	built or builded	built or builded
burst	burst	burst
catch	caught	caught

Irregular Verbs (continued)

Present	Past	Past Participle
choose	chose	chosen
come	came	come
cost	cost	cost
creep	crept	crept
cut	cut	cut
dig	dug	dug
dive	dived or dove	dived
do	did	done
draw	drew	drawn
dream	dreamed or dreamt	dreamed or dreamt
drink	drank	drunk
drive	drove	driven
eat	ate	eaten
fall	fell	fallen
feed	fed	fed
feel	felt	felt
fight	fought	fought
fly	flew	flown
forbid	forbade	forbidden
forget	forgot	forgotten
forgive	forgave	forgiven
freeze	froze	frozen
get	got	got or gotten
give	gave	given
go	went	gone
grow	grew	grown
grind	ground	ground
hang	hung or hanged	hung
has	had	had
hear	heard	heard
hide	hid	hidden
hold	held	held
hurt	hurt	hurt
is	was	has been
keep	kept	kept
kneel	kneeled or knelt	kneeled or knelt
know	knew	known
lay	laid	laid
leap	leaped or leapt	leaped or leapt
leave	left	left
lend	lent	lent
let	let	let
lie	lay	lain
light	lit	lit
lose	lost	lost
make	made	made
mean	meant	meant
mow	mowed	mowed or mown
put	put	put
read	read	read
ride	rode	ridden
ring	rang	rung
rise	rose	risen
run	ran	run
say	said	said

Present	Past	Past Participle
saw	sawed	sawed or sawn
see	saw	seen
sell	sold	sold
sew	sewed	sewed or sewn
set	set	set
shake	shook	shaken
shed	shed	shed
shine	shined or shone	shined or shone
shoot	shot	shot
show	showed	shown or showed
shrink	shrank or shrunk	shrunk
shut	shut	shut
sing	sang	sung
sink	sank	sunk
sit	sat	sat
sleep	slept	slept
slide	slid	slid
sow	sowed	sowed or sown
speak	spoke	spoken
spend	spent	spent
spin	spun	spun
split	split	split
spread	spread	spread
spring	sprang or sprung	sprung
stand	stood	stood
steal	stole	stolen
stick	stuck	stuck
sting	stung	stung
strike	struck	struck
string	strung	strung
spit	spit	spit
sweat	sweat or sweated	sweat or sweated
sweep	swept	swept
swear	swore	sworn
swim	swam or swum	swum
swing	swung or swang	swung
take	took	taken
teach	taught	taught
tear	tore	torn
tell	told	told
think	thought	thought
throw	threw	thrown
understand	understood	understood
wake	woke or waked	woken or waked
wear	wore	worn
weave	wove	woven
weep	wept	wept
wet	wet	wet
win	won	won
wind	wound	wound
write	wrote	written

List 12: Irregular Plurals

"The men chased the mice into the woods."

OBJECTIVE

To develop the student's ability to identify and use correct plural forms in functional language.

APPLICATIONS

♦ Teach the rule for forming each set of irregular plurals. Teach similar groups together (e.g., f or fe to ves).

♦ Students can find or draw pictures to illustrate irregular verbs. Combine these in a mini-book.

♦ Have the student tell mini-stories to practice the plural forms. Make up stories with the children using as many of the irregular plural forms as possible. Make flannelboard characters to go with them and let the children retell them. (Use men, women, children, wolves, mice, thieves, sheep, police, cattle, etc.) See illustration.

The students can tell the stories to other groups of students or to children in lower grades.

Add *es* to words ending in *ss, z, sh, ch, x*

tax	taxes
waltz	waltzes
glass	glasses
switch	switches
wish	wishes
(etc.)	

Change *y* to *i* and add *es*

sky	skies
fly	flies
(etc.)	

Change *f* or *fe* to *v* and add *es*

leaf	leaves
elf	elves
shelf	shelves
thief	thieves
wolf	wolves
half	halves
calf	calves
loaf	loaves
self	selves
knife	knives
wife	wives
life	lives

Major spelling change

goose	geese
mouse	mice

man	men
woman	women
child	children
louse	lice
foot	feet
tooth	teeth

Constant Form

deer	deer
fish	fish (or fishes)
sheep	sheep
reindeer	reindeer
buffalo	buffalo
moose	moose
spaghetti	spaghetti

Intrinsic Plural Form

pants	pliers
scissors	trousers
stilts	shorts
clothes	glasses
spectacles	police
binoculars	cattle

Plural in Form but Singular in Meaning

mumps	economics
news	series
mathematics	woods
measles	gallows
physics	species

Lists 13–14: Prefixes and Suffixes

OBJECTIVE

To develop the student's ability to identify and understand the meanings of affixes and subsequently decode the words they appear in.

APPLICATIONS

◆ Explain the meaning of the prefix or suffix. Brainstorm all the words with that affix and write them on a chart. Talk about the meanings of the words and use in sentences.

◆ Have students look in newspapers or magazines and find words with prefixes or suffixes. Cut the words out and paste in mini-books as parts of new sentences they write.

compl_iant_   defi_ant_

List 13: Prefixes and Combining Forms

Prefix	Meaning	Examples
abs	from	absent, abstract
ad, ap, at	to	advance, approach, attack
*auto	self	automatic, automobile
bi	two	bicycle, bifocal
*bio	life	biology, biomedical
com, con, col	with	combine, confront, collect
de	from, undo	depart, defrost
dis	apart	disappoint, disassociate, disagree
en	put into or on	enclose, envelope, enthrone
ex	out of, former, from	export, exchange
in, im, em	into, in	inside, imbed, empower, embalm
inter	between	interact, intersperse
in, im, ir	not	indirect, imperfect, indecent, immature irreplaceable, irregular
*micro	small	microscope, microphone
mis	wrong	misspell, mistake
ob, op	against	obstruct, oppress
*para	at the side of	parallel, paramedic
*photo	produced by light	photograph, photostat
pre	before	precede, prevent, prepaid
*poly	many	polygamy, polytechnical
pro	move forward, before	project, proceed, propose
re	back	reappear, recall, refresh
sub	under	submarine, subnormal
*tele	at a distance	telegram, telephone
*trans	across or above	transport, transcontinental
tri	three	tricycle, triangle
un	back, not	untie, unfold, uncork, unhappy, unchanged

*combining forms

List 14: Suffixes

Suffix	Meaning	Examples
able, ible	capable of, worthy	agreeable, comfortable, credible
age	act or state of	salvage, bondage
acy, isy	quality of	hypocrisy, piracy
al, eal, ial	on account of, related to, the action of	judicial, official arrival, refusal
ance, ence	act or fact of doing, state of	violence, dependence allowance, insurance
ant	quality of, one who	defiant, expectant, reliant occupant, accountant
er, or	agent, one who	author, baker, winner
ed	past	jumped, baked
ery	a place to, practice of, condition	nunnery, cannery surgery bravery, drudgery
dom	state, condition of	wisdom, kingdom, martyrdom
ent	having the quality of	different, dependent, innocent, insistent
en	made of, to make	woolen, wooden, darken
eur, er, or	one who	dictator, chauffeur, worker
er	degree of comparison	harder, newer, older
est	highest degree of comparison	cleanest, hardest, softest
ful	full of	graceful, restful, faithful
hood	state of being	boyhood, knighthood, womanhood
ible, ile, il	capable of being	digestible, responsible, docile, civil
ier, ior	one who	carrier, warrior
ify	to make	magnify, beautify, falsify
ic	like, made of	metallic, toxic, poetic
ing	action of	running, wishing
ion	act or state of	confusion, correction, protection
ism	fact of being	communism, socialism
ish	like	childish, sheepish, foolish
ist	a person who does	artist, geologist
ity, ty	state of	majesty, chastity, humanity
*itis	inflammation of	appendicitis, tonsillitis
ive	having nature of	attractive, active
ize	to make	pasteurize, motorize
less	without	motionless, careless, childless
let	small	starlet, eaglet

*combining forms

Suffix	Meaning	Examples
ly	like, in a manner, happening every	heavenly, remarkably, suddenly, absolutely, monthly
ment	state or quality, act of doing	accomplishment, excitement placement, movement
*meter	device for measuring	thermometer, barometer
ness	state of	blindness, kindness
*ology	study of	geology, zoology, archaeology
ous, ious	full of	joyous, marvelous, furious
ship	quality or state of, rank of	friendship, leadership governorship, lordship
*scope	instrument for seeing	telescope, microscope
some	like	tiresome, lonesome
tion, sion	action, state of being	condition, attention, fusion
ty	quality or state of	liberty, majesty
ward	toward	southward, forward
y	like, full of, action of, diminutive, endearing	noisy, sooty, jealousy inquiry kitty, Billy

*combining forms

Lists 15–16: Scrambled Sentences

OBJECTIVE

To develop the student's ability to recognize and use correct word order in sentences.

APPLICATIONS

♦ Make up cards with the scrambled sentences on them (see illustration). Read the words. Students rearrange the words and say the sentence in correct order.

♦ Present the scrambled sentence orally. Students must rearrange words and say them in a proper sentence.

♦ Students can make up their own sentences to try out on the class or group.

♦ *Note:* Some sentences may be arranged in two different orders.

Example: We can't win.
Can't we win?

List 15: Scrambled 3-Word Sentences

1. monsters I like
2. mean are bears
3. werewolf the howls
4. creaks door the
5. silly you are
6. popsicles yummy are
7. scare people vampires
8. melts cream ice
9. he goodby said
10. jump high fish
11. am sleepy I
12. candy likes she
13. are fun parties
14. dogs bones chew
15. feet my hurt
16. birds worms eat
17. lay eggs chickens
18. scary lightning is
19. elephants trunks have
20. swim I fast
21. boo ghosts say
22. crackles the fire
23. soft kitties are

24. bunnies sniff little
25. am scared I
26. can't win we
27. bright lights are
28. fun are puppets
29. pick cherries we
30. I comics read
31. laughed hard John
32. expensive are milkshakes
33. Disneyland like I
34. bubblegum chew I
35. sunburned don't get
36. cake a bake
37. is Christmas when
38. play football let's
39. birds fly do
40. the piano play
41. Maria win could
42. you tired aren't
43. the secret tell
44. songs I sing
45. loud scream don't
46. funny Snoopy is

47. dog your feed
48. Santa come will
49. strong is Batman
50. Snoopy is where
51. horn your blow
52. Monopoly play let's
53. monster the walks
54. stand please up
55. nose your touch
56. to sleep go
57. ate cookies Goofy
58. throw don't rocks
59. you sing will
60. the beach where's
61. your snap fingers
62. tigers for watch
63. play football let's
64. dream you do
65. police call the
66. swim can you
67. for me smile
68. real are ghosts
69. buy toys I
70. dad here comes
71. porridge ate Goldilocks
72. stink skunks little
73. a take shower

74. my broke bicycle
75. crashed plane the
76. helps people Superman
77. hurts tooth my
78. me scare mice
79. the flies bird
80. let's bubbles blow
81. bony are skeletons
82. do tricks clowns
83. are coming you
84. Julie mad is
85. is Bill where
86. ring bell the
87. jumps my dog
88. paints Juan pictures
89. eat peanuts elephants
90. my that's football
91. pack suitcase the
92. hamburgers Jack eats
93. sticky gum is
94. swims Jeff fast
95. play I pingpong
96. the popped popcorn
97. pencil broke my
98. soft are pillows
99. him hit Billy
100. diapers wear babies

List 16: Scrambled 4-Word Sentences

1. can ice I skate
2. my is popsicle cold
3. pickles like do you
4. fifty eggs colored I
5. my monkey is this
6. eats the shark fish
7. down Humpty fell Dumpty
8. shoe her lost Cinderella
9. bears Goldilocks three saw
10. carrots likes Bunny Bugs
11. saw we outside fireworks
12. Lincoln slaves freed Abraham
13. rockets the off blast
14. shipwrecked Robinson Crusoe was
15. furry my rabbit is
16. live rattlesnakes in holes
17. animals circus are elephants
18. cats kittens mother have
19. dogs pets are good
20. baseball boys ten played
21. eats a bird worms
22. is circus the coming
23. has werewolf the fangs
24. Mouse is Mickey funny
25. a Bambi fawn is
26. fiction science interesting is
27. like you do candy
28. do tricks magicians can
29. very sharks are dangerous
30. motorcycles like I riding
31. a KingKong gorilla is
32. presents us Santa brings
33. my broken is yoyo
34. send you do Valentines
35. fast skateboard my goes
36. when your is birthday
37. six I puppets have
38. a judo is sport
39. weird that fish is
40. a let's have picnic
41. a holiday Thanksgiving is
42. your where are dolls
43. landed the plane safely
44. injured was driver the
45. got boys the cokes
46. car I the washed
47. the Billy made sandwiches
48. people vote will most
49. pretty are you very
50. hot we pizza ate
51. cut I my toe
52. the is bright campfire
53. doughnuts chocolate I like
54. you like do fudge
55. the down house burned
56. saw a clown I
57. flashlight your where is
58. first Pete won prize
59. loud is thunder the
60. very much you thank
61. take home me please
62. is finished my work
63. sailboats the fast are
64. puppies to chew like
65. mail letter my please

List 17: Constructing Sentences

OBJECTIVE

To develop the student's ability to use correct inflections in saying declarative, interrogative and exclamatory sentences and to compose these types of sentences.

A ghost said "Boo!"

APPLICATIONS

♦ Discuss sentence types and punctuation. Discuss inflection of voice in response to sentence types. Have students read some examples.

♦ Let students choose a subject such as *spaceships* from List 17. The student gives one declarative sentence, one interrogative and one exclamatory related to the subject. This can be done as an individual, group or class exercise. The student may write the sentences or dictate to the specialist. An imperative sentence may also be added.

Example: *Spaceships*

I sure like spaceships!
Have you ever been in one?
I saw one in the sky.

Disneyland

Have you been to Disneyland?
I went to a haunted house there.
A ghost said "Boo!"
Go to Disneyland soon.

Topics for 3 sentences (declarative, interrogative, exclamatory)

1. spaceships
2. Disneyland
3. cats
4. monsters
5. Christmas
6. skeletons
7. painting
8. elephants
9. fire
10. giants
11. rain
12. bugs
13. earthquake
14. music
15. horses
16. swimming
17. circus
18. baseball
19. zoo
20. desserts
21. racing cars
22. clowns
23. movies
24. the moon
25. television

26. dentist
27. camping
28. space travel
29. 4th of July
30. Superman
31. popsicles
32. babies
33. vacation
34. accident
35. trampoline
36. President _____
37. a wish
38. jungle
39. a dream
40. magic
41. fishing
42. prize
43. haunted house
44. dogs
45. pickles
46. lightning
47. pigs
48. astronauts
49. firemen
50. gardens

List 18: Contractions

OBJECTIVE

To develop the student's ability to identify and use correct contraction forms in functional language.

APPLICATIONS

* Make cards with the contracted form (I'm) on one side and the regular form (I am) on the other. The student draws a card and uses the contracted form in a sentence, and gives the regular form.

* Have the student write a story using as many of the contractions as possible. He may read the story and the other students write down all the contractions they hear.

I	we	you/you (pl)	he/she/it	they
I'm	we're	you're	he's	they're
I'll	we'll	you'll	he'll	they'll
I've	we've	you've	he's	they've
I'd	we'd	you'd	he'd	they'd
(I'm not)	aren't	aren't	isn't	aren't
can't	can't	can't	can't	can't
don't	don't	don't	doesn't	don't
didn't	didn't	didn't	didn't	didn't
haven't	haven't	haven't	haven't	haven't
won't	won't	won't	won't	won't
wouldn't	wouldn't	wouldn't	wouldn't	wouldn't
couldn't	couldn't	couldn't	couldn't	couldn't
shouldn't	shouldn't	shouldn't	shouldn't	shouldn't
wasn't	weren't	weren't	wasn't	weren't
mustn't	mustn't	mustn't	mustn't	mustn't
hadn't	hadn't	hadn't	hadn't	hadn't

Interrogatives

who's	what's	when's	where's
who'll	what'll	who'd	where'll

Other

there's	that's	here's
there'll	that'll	
let's		

III. Meaning of Language (semantics and comprehension)

Idioms: throw a party

19. Basic concepts
20. Basic concept activities
21. Compound words
22. Compound word activity
23. Homophones, level 1
24. Homophones, level 2
25. Homophones, level 3
26. Homographs
27. Heteronyms
28. Antonyms, level 1
29. Antonyms, level 2
30. Antonyms, level 3
31. Adjectives
32. Adverbs
33. Adverb activity
34. Abbreviation
35. Similes

36. Idioms, food and colors
37. Idioms, animals
38. Idioms, parts of the body
39. Idioms, miscellaneous
40. Proverbs
41. Scrambled 2-sentence sequence
42. Scrambled 3-sentence sequence
43. Incomplete sentences, level 1
44. Incomplete sentences, level 2
45. Incomplete sentences, level 3
46. Incomplete sentences, level 4
47. Following 2 directions
48. Following 3 directions
49. Giving and following directions
50. Synonyms, level 1
51. Synonyms, level 2

Lists 19–20: Basic Concepts

OBJECTIVE

To develop the student's ability to understand and use basic concept words in meaningful contexts.

APPLICATIONS

* Teach each group of concepts together using body movements.

  Example: in-out, inside-outside, inside out, into

  An obstacle course or playground may be used to teach many of the concepts. Use a lot of commentary as students do activities. "John is going *into* the pipe." "Anita is hiding *outside* the monkey bars." "Julie is *in* the *middle*."

  Use the same concept words often during the day.

over/under/in

* List 20 has specific directions for using the spatial concepts on List 19.

* Use small objects or toys that the children can manipulate and talk about to teach concepts. Children love them.

  Example: "Put the dog *in* the purse." "Where is the football now?" (*inside* the box) "Which baby is *bigger*?"

* Construct analogies to reinforce Basic Concepts.

  Example: A building is *high;* a sidewalk is _____.
  A car is *heavy;* a feather is _____.

List 19: Basic Concepts

SPATIAL

A. above — below
   over — under
   underneath
   overhead

B. next to — away from
   beside
   by
   against
   close to
   near — far
   together — apart
   separated
   toward — away from
   to — from
   here — there
   at
   facing

C. front — back
   in front of — in back of
   ahead — behind
   forward — backward
   sideways
   before — after

D. in — out
   inside — outside
   inside out
   into
   on — off

E. top — bottom
   on top of
   up — down
   upside down
   high — low
   sides

F. middle — center
   between
   through
   across
   around

G. in a row
   in order
   1st, 2nd, 3rd
   first — middle — last
   beginning — middle — end

H. corner
   right — left

31

Basic Concepts (continued)

QUANTITATIVE

equal — unequal
same as — different from
as many as — as few as
as much as — as little as

most — least
more — less
several — few
many — some
all — none — zero
whole — part
half

some — more — most
small — middle sized — large
big — bigger — biggest
little — big
short — tall
short — long
thin — thick
skinny — fat
narrow — wide
heavy — light

pair
couple
both

empty — full
almost
enough — too much
every

TEMPORAL

never — always
sometimes — often
almost

first — second — third
beginning — middle — end
finish
first — last
before — after
early — late
now — later

young — old
slow — fast
yesterday — today —
    tomorrow

OTHER

like
alike
match
same — different

good — better — best
bad — worse — worst

smooth — rough
straight — crooked
open — closed
flat
old — new
with — without
turn off — turn on
take away from
skip
doesn't have

List 20: Basic Concept Activities

Equipment needed: 1 hula hoop, 3 chairs (different sizes if possible), 1 cardboard box, 1 board (6 in. x 2 ft. or longer), 1 pillow, 1 beanbag, books, chalk.

The first part of each direction set may be performed indoors or outdoors. The second set of directions may be used if space is not available, if children are immobile, or as a second exercise.

The directions are matched to the sets of spatial concepts on List 19, Basic Concepts.

A. 1. Jump *over* the board.
Put your hands *over* your head.

2. Put the beanbag *under* a chair.
Put your finger *under* your chin.

3. Put the pillow *overhead.*
Put your fist *overhead.*

4. Put the beanbag *underneath* the pillow.
Put your finger *underneath* your ear.

5. Put your hands *above* the box.
Put your hand *above* your shoulder.

6. Put your foot *below* a chair.
Put your thumb *below* your elbow.

B. 1. Stand *beside* the box.
Put your book *beside* the desk.

2. Put the beanbag *near* the chair.
Put your tongue *near* your finger.

3. Hop *from* the chair *to* the hoop.
Slide your finger *from* your hand *to* your elbow.

4. Put the chairs *together.*
Put your knees *together.*

5. *Separate* the chairs.
Separate your fingers.

6. Put the pillow *against* the board.
Put your hand *against* your cheek.

7. Place the beanbag *close to* the box.
Put your book *close to* your leg.

8. Sit *next to* the box.
Put your thumb *next to* your ear.

9. Walk *away from* the board.
   Hold your hand *away from* your face.

10. Put the pillow *far from* the board.
    Hold the book *far from* your toes.

11. Jump *toward* the board.
    Make your finger go *toward* your tummy.

12. Take the pillow *to* the chair.
    Point *to* the hoop.

13. Put the beanbag *here.* (Point to the direction.)

14. Put the pillow *there.* (Point to the direction.)

15. Sit *facing* the chair.
    Face the window.

C. 1. Make a 1 *on the front* of the box with chalk.
    Make a 1 *on the front* of your book.

2. Make a 2 *on the back* of the box with chalk.
   Put your hand *on the back* of your neck.

3. Stand *behind* the big chair.
   Put your hands *behind* your head.

4. Walk *sideways* to the hoop.
   Move your arm *sideways.*

5. Kneel *in front of* the pillow.
   Put your hand *in front of* your chair.

6. Hide *in back of* the box.
   Put your fist *in back of* your elbow.

7. Bend *forward* and touch the board.
   Move your foot *forward.*

8. Walk *backward* to the box.
   Move your head *backward.*

D. 1. Put the pillow *on* the chair.
    Put your fist *on* your knee.

2. Take the pillow *off* the chair.
   Take your shoe *off.*

3. Stand *inside* the hoop.

   Put your finger *inside* the book.

4. Stand *outside* of the hoop.

   Put your finger *outside* of your shoe.

5. Put the beanbag *in* the box.

   Put your finger *in* your mouth.

6. Take the beanbag *out* of the box.

   Take the paper *out* of the book.

7. Walk *into* the hoop.

   Throw the beanbag *into* the box.

E. 1. Put the pillow *on top of* the chair.

    Put your finger *on top of* your head.

2. Touch the *bottom* of the chair.

   Touch the *bottom* of your foot.

3. Push the pillow *up* the side of the box.

   Point *up* to the ceiling.

4. Drop the beanbag *down* the side of the box.

   Look *down* at the floor.

5. Hold the pillow *high* over the hoop.

   Put your hand *high* over your shoulder.

6. Throw the beanbag *low* across the floor.

   Swing your hand *low* over the table.

F. 1. Walk *across* the board.

    Put your hand *across* your other hand.

2. Put the beanbag in the *center* of the hoop.

   Touch the *center* of your stomach.

3. Skip *around* the hoop.

   Move your hand *around* your head.

4. Stand in the *middle* of the hoop.

   Put your finger in the *middle* of the book.

5. Walk *between* the chairs.

   Put the book *between* your hands.

6. Go *through* the hoop.

   Put your finger *through* your hair.

Basic Concept Activities (continued)

Needed: three pencils of different sizes and paper.

        G. 1. Put the chairs *in a row*.
              Put the pencils *in a row*.

             2. Put the beanbag on the *middle* chair.
              Take away the *middle* pencil.

             3. Sit in the *first* chair.
              Pick up the *first* pencil.

             4. Put the pillow on the *last* chair.
              Write with the *last* pencil on the paper.

             5. Put the chairs *in order* from smallest to largest.
              Put the pencils *in order* from smallest to largest.

As you do the activities, ask questions to stimulate verbal use of the concepts:

    Where is the beanbag?

    What is next to the board?

    Are the chairs together or apart?

    What is farthest from the chair?

    Where are you sitting?

    Where is Bill going?

    Is he going forward or backward?

Lists 21–22: Compound Words

OBJECTIVE

To develop the student's ability to recognize compound words, decipher their meanings by analyzing their parts and use them in meaningful language.

APPLICATIONS

♦ Discuss the meaning of each word part and of the whole compound word. Students can make folding cards (see illustration) with pictures of the two combined words on the front flaps and the compound word inside. Sets of these can be used with other students. The pictures can either be drawn or cut from workbooks, magazines or comic strips.

♦ Some of the compound words on the lists are marked by asterisks. On a 5 x 7 card write the first part of one of these words and leave lines for the student to fill in other words that would complete the compound word. Put the answers on the back and laminate the front of the cards so they may be used repeatedly. On List 22 the combinations of the selected words are listed.

♦ Print the first parts of fifteen compound words on index card strips. Print the second parts on colored card strips. The student matches up the cards to make compound words.

♦ Have students find compound words while "hunting" through reading material and make lists. Use the words in new sentences.

♦ Write compound words on small cards. Two students must <u>pantomime</u> the word parts consecutively and the others guess the compound word.

♦ Give each student a short list of compound words. Read sentences leaving out a compound word and have students find and say the appropriate word.

List 21: Compound Words

afternoon	bankbook	blackbird	cakepan
*airmail	barefoot	blowout	campfire
airplane	barnyard	blueberry	candlestick
airport	baseball	boardwalk	cardboard
anybody	basketball	boathouse	carefree
anything	bathrobe	*bookkeeper	caretaker
applesauce	bathroom	bookmark	*carsick
ashcan	bathtub	bookstore	chairman
babysit	bedroom	bookworm	chalkboard
*backbone	bedtime	boxcar	churchmouse
backpack	beehive	brainstorm	copyright
backrub	bellbottom	breadbox	cornerstone
backstop	billboard	breakfast	cornfield
backstroke	billfold	bricklayer	countdown
bagpipe	birdhouse	bridegroom	countryside
*ballgame	birthplace	bullfight	courtroom
ballplayer	birthday	bunkhouse	cowbell

37

Compound Words (continued)

cowboy	flypaper	landowner
cowpoke	*football	lawbreaker
crossroad	footprint	lawnchair
crossword	footstool	launchpad
crybaby	fruitcake	letdown
cufflink	gentleman	lifeboat
cupcake	goalkeeper	lifeguard
daredevil	godmother	lifelike
darkroom	goldfish	lifesaver
daydream	grandfather	lifesize
daylight	grapevine	lifetime
dishpan	grasshopper	lighthouse
dishcloth	greenhouse	lookout
dishwasher	groundhog	lunchroom
doghouse	guidebook	mailbox
doorbell	gumdrop	mailman
doorman	gunfire	mainland
doorstep	gunpowder	masterpiece
downhill	hairbrush	matchbook
downpour	haircut	meatloaf
downstairs	hairline	mixup
downstream	halftime	moonlight
dressmaker	hallway	motorcycle
driveway	*handbag	mountaintop
drugstore	handball	mouthpiece
drumstick	handcuff	nameless
dustpan	handwriting	nearby
duststorm	hatrack	newspaper
earache	*headache	newsstand
eardrum	headlight	nightgown
earmuff	headrest	nightmare
earphone	heavyweight	nosebleed
earring	henhouse	noseplugs
eggnog	highchair	nutcracker
eggplant	highway	nutshell
eggshell	hilltop	oatmeal
evergreen	*homemade	offside
everything	hometown	oilcan
eyeball	homework	*overhead
eyeglass	horseback	oversee
eyelid	horserace	oversleep
fairground	houseboat	overweight
farmhouse	housedog	outcast
farmyard	indoors	outfield
farsighted	infield	pancake
featherweight	instep	pantleg
fingernail	junkyard	*paperback
fingerprint	Junebug	pickup
*fireman	kettledrum	pinecone
fireplace	keychain	pinwheel
fisherman	keyhole	pitchfork
fishhook	knockout	playground
fishpond	ladybug	playmate
flagpole	lamppost	playroom
flashlight	lampshade	policeman
flowerpot	landmark	popcorn

prizefighter
quicksand
racehorse
railroad
rainbow
raincoat
reindeer
riverboat
*roommate
rosebud
rosebush
roundhouse
roundup
sailboat
salesman
sandbox
sandpaper
sawmill
scarecrow
schoolhouse
scoreboard
seaport
seatcover
sellout
setup
*shoelace
shoemaker
shoeskates
shoestring
shortcut
shortstop
singalong
skateboard
skyline
skyscraper
smokestack

snowflake
snowman
snowplow
snowstorm
songwriter
soupbone
spaceman
spaceship
sparerib
starfish
starlight
steamship
stepladder
stepson
stomachache
storybook
streetcar
suitcase
summertime
sunburn
sunflower
sunlight
supermarket
surfboard
teacup
teaspoon
teenage
textbook
Thanksgiving
thunderstorm
timeclock
tiptoe
toadstool
toothache
toothbrush

toothpaste
topcoat
tophat
touchdown
trademark
treehouse
typewriter
*underground
undertaker
underwear
underweight
uproot
upstage
upstairs
waistband
waistline
wallpaper
warehouse
warship
wastebasket
*watercolor
waterfall
waterproof
waterski
weathervane
weekend
whirlpool
whirlwind
widespread
windmill
windstorm
vineyard
yardstick
yearbook
zookeeper

List 22: Compound Word Activities

AIR
airbrush
aircool
aircraft
airmail
airplane
airport
airraid
airship
airtight

BACK
backbone
backdrop
backfield
backfire
background
backhand
backpack
backrub
backstage
backstop
backstroke
backwash
backwoods
fullback
halfback

BALL
ballgame
ballpark
ballplayer
ballroom
baseball
basketball
eyeball
football
handball

BOOK
bookend
bookkeeper
bookmaker
bookrack
bookseller
bookshelf
bookstore
bankbook
guidebook
matchbook
storybook
yearbook

CAR
carfare
carload
carport
carseat

carsick
boxcar
streetcar

FIRE
firebox
firebug
firecracker
firefly
fireman
fireplug
fireplace
fireproof
fireside
firewood
fireworks
campfire

FOOT
football
foothill
foothold
footlights
footman
footnote
footpath
footprint
footrest
footstep
footwork
barefoot

HAND
handbag
handball
handbill
handbook
handcuff
handout
handshake
handspring
handwork
handwriting
backhand
forehand
farmhand

HEAD
headache
headboard
headdress
headhunter
headgear
headless
headlight
headline
headmaster
headphone

headquarters
headrest
headstone
headstrong
headwaiter
overhead
redhead

HOME
homecoming
homeland
homemade
homeplate
homeroom
homerun
homesick
homestretch
hometown
homework

LIGHT
lightbulb
lighthouse
lightweight
lightyear
daylight
flashlight
headlight
moonlight
starlight
moonlight

OVER
overbid
overcharge
overcoat
overdose
overflow
overgrow
overhand
overhead
overhear
overlook
overpass
overseas
oversee
overshoe
oversleep
overthrow
overtime
overweight
pushover
walkover

PAPER
paperboy
paperback
paperweight

flypaper
newspaper
sandpaper
wallpaper

ROOM
roommate
bathroom
bedroom
classroom
courtroom
darkroom
lunchroom
playroom

SHOE
shoehorn
shoelace
shoemaker
shoeshine
shoestore
shoestring
horseshoe

UNDER
underarm
underbid
undercharge
underclothes
undercover
underfoot
undergraduate
underground
underhand
underpass
underpay
undersea
undershirt
underwater
underwear
underwrite

WATER
waterbed
watercolor
waterfall
watermark
watermelon
waterproof
watershed
waterski
waterspout
watertight
rainwater
seawater
underwater

Lists 23–25: Homophones

NOTE: According to the *Random House Dictionary of the English Language:**

a *homophone* is "a word pronounced the same as, but differing in meaning from another, whether spelled the same or not . . ." (bare — bear);

a *homograph* is "a word of the same written form as another but of different origin and meaning. . ." (buck, buck);

a *heteronym* is "a word having a different sound and meaning from another but the same spelling. . ." (mińute — unit of time; minuté — very small).

He could not tie a knot.

OBJECTIVE

To develop the student's ability to recognize the different meanings of homophone pairs and use the words appropriately in functional language.

APPLICATIONS

♦ Each sentence illustrating a homophone on this list gives a clue to the meaning.

Example: The prisoner is in the (jail) *cell.*
Do you *sell* popcorn for (fifteen cents)?

♦ Talk about the difference in meanings of the words in the sentences.

♦ Write selected homophone pairs on cards. Students draw cards and act out the words while others guess the pairs (bare — bear). The guesser uses the words in sentences to describe what the actors are doing.

Example: John has *bare* feet.
Mickey is a ferocious *bear.*

♦ Give the students lists of homophone pairs. The students use both words in one sentence.

Example: The *doe* ate some bread *dough.*

♦ Students can draw pictures of the homophones on a tagboard strip, printing the words on the reverse side. Other students can guess the pairs.

♦ Make riddles: "What word means *to hit* and *a red vegetable?*" (beat — beet)

List 23: Level I

1. ATE   I *ate* two hotdogs.
   EIGHT   Pete is *eight* years old.

2. BARE   I walked in the water with *bare* feet.
   BEAR   The grizzly *bear* is black.

3. BEAT   Tom *beat* the drum.
   BEET   A *beet* is a red vegetable.

Random House Dictionary of the English Language, The Unabridged Edition, Jess Stein, Editor in Chief. New York: Random House, Inc., 1973.

4. BE   Will you *be* home tonight?
    BEE   The *bee* is buzzing.

5. BREAK   Don't *break* my toy.
    BRAKE   Put your foot on the *brake* in the car.

6. BLEW   The wind *blew* hard.
    BLUE   The water in the pool is *blue*.

7. BOARD   The carpenter is sawing the *board*.
    BORED   I was *bored* at the movie.

8. BUY   Let's *buy* some bubble gum.
    BY   Juan stood *by* the clown.

9. CELL   The prisoner is in the jail *cell*.
    SELL   Do you *sell* popcorn?

10. CENT   The lollipop costs one *cent*.
     SENT   My grandpa *sent* me a present.
     SCENT   The *scent* of the perfume is nice.

11. CHEAP   These marbles were very *cheap*.
     CHEEP   I can hear the birds *cheep*.

12. CLOSE   Please *close* the door.
     CLOTHES   Pack your *clothes* in the suitcase.

13. DEAR   The witch said, ''Come here, my *dear*.''
     DEER   The *deer* ran through the forest.

14. DEW   The *dew* on the grass got my shoes wet.
     DO   Will you *do* me a favor?
     DUE   Your library book is *due*.

15. DIE   The insect will *die* after it stings.
     DYE   I will *dye* my T-shirt yellow.

16. DOE   The *doe* took care of her fawn.
     DOUGH   We made bread *dough*.

17. FAIR   We must play *fair*. The State *Fair* is coming.
     FARE   How much is the plane *fare?*

18. FIR   We cut down a *fir* tree at Christmastime.
     FUR   The skunk has black and white *fur*.

19. FLEA   The dog has a *flea* on his back.
     FLEE   The soldiers will *flee* from the enemy.

20. FLU   Jack is sick with the *flu.*

      FLUE   The smoke went up the chimney *flue.*

      FLEW   The robin *flew* to her nest.

21. FLOUR   Put two cups of *flour* in the cake batter.

      FLOWER   The rose is a beautiful *flower.*

22. FOR   This present is *for* you.

      FORE   The golfer yelled *"fore"* before he hit the ball.

      FOUR   My brother is *four* years old.

23. HALL   We walked down the *hall.*

      HAUL   Dad will *haul* the trash to the dump.

24. HAY   My horse eats *hay.*

      HEY   *Hey!* Don't do that!

25. HEAL   That cut will *heal* quickly.

      HEEL   My *heel* is below my ankle.

26. HEAR   Did you *hear* the good news?

      HERE   Superman is coming *here.*

27. IN   Put the puppy *in* the box.

      INN   We stayed overnight at an *inn.*

28. KNOT   Tie a *knot* in that rope.

      NOT   I am *not* sleepy.

29. KNOW   I *know* my math facts.

      NO   Bill has *no* money.

30. LEAD   *Lead* is a very heavy metal.

      LED   The seeing–eye dog *led* his master.

31. MAIL   Did I get any *mail* today?

      MALE   A buck is a *male* deer.

32. MEAT   Have you eaten deer *meat?*

      MEET   Joe will *meet* us at the movie.

33. NEW   Your *new* yoyo is neat.

      KNEW   My dad *knew* the president.

      GNU   The *gnu* looks like a buffalo.

34. NOSE   My *nose* got sunburned.

      KNOWS   Jill *knows* all the answers.

35. PAIL   Fill the *pail* with water.

      PALE   You look *pale* when you are sick.

36. PAIR   I got a *pair* of jogging shoes.

      PARE   Please *pare* the potatoes.

      PEAR   The *pear* is a delicious yellow fruit.

37. PEACE   There is *peace* and quiet in the country.

      PIECE   Would you like a *piece* of cake?

38. PEAK   We climbed up to the *peak* of the mountain.

      PEEK   Don't *peek* at the presents!

39. PLAIN   I like *plain* doughnuts.

      PLANE   Have you flown on a *plane?*

40. RAIN   The *rain* made big puddles.

      REIN   I pulled the *rein* to make the horse stop.

      REIGN   The king will *reign* over his country.

41. READ   Have you *read* "Cinderella?"

      RED   I ate a juicy *red* apple.

42. REAL   Are those *real* diamonds?

      REEL   Paul has a new rod and *reel* for fishing.

43. RIGHT   My *right* hand is broken.

      RITE   The elves performed a *rite.*

      WRITE   Anita will *write* a letter to her mom.

44. ROAD   This *road* is bumpy.

      RODE   We *rode* our new bicycles.

      ROWED   Jack and Jill *rowed* the boat.

45. SAIL   Put up the *sail* on the boat.

      SALE   Ice cream is on *sale* at the store.

46. SEA   The pirates sailed on the *sea.*

      SEE   Can you *see* your friends?

47. SEAM   I sewed the side *seam* on my pants.

      SEEM   You *seem* to be tired.

48. SEW   Pearl will *sew* on her new sewing machine.

      SO   I am *so* tired.

      SOW   The farmer will *sow* the seeds.

49. SON   The queen had a baby *son.*

      SUN   The *sun* is a star.

50. STEAL   The thief tried to *steal* the money.

      STEEL   My bike is made of *steel.*

51. TACKS — We pounded *tacks* into the board.

    TAX — My dad pays income *tax.*

52. TAIL — The horse has a long *tail.*

    TALE — "Sleeping Beauty" is a fairy *tale.*

53. THREW — The pitcher *threw* the ball.

    THROUGH — The basketball went *through* the hoop.

List 24: Level II

1. AID — I will *aid* you with your homework.

   AIDE — The President's *aide* helps him with his duties.

2. AISLE — The bride walked down the *aisle* of the church.

   I'LL — *I'll* take you to the circus.

   ISLE — An *isle* is a small island.

3. BAIL — We had to *bail* out the water from the boat.
   The man had to pay *bail* to get out of jail.

   BALE — The horse ate a whole *bale* of hay.

4. BALD — The man's head was *bald.*

   BAWLED — The baby *bawled* very loudly.

5. BERRY — The red *berry* tasted good.

   BURY — The poodle will *bury* his bone.

6. BEACH — Lucy built a sand castle on the *beach.*

   BEECH — The birds built a nest in the *beech* tree.

7. BOUGH — The *bough* of the tree broke.

   BOW — You must *bow* before the audience.

8. BURRO — The boy rode the *burro* down the canyon.

   BURROW — Some animals *burrow* into the ground.

9. BRAID — Rosie can *braid* her hair.

   BRAYED — The donkey *brayed* very loudly.

10. BRIDAL — Nancy wore her *bridal* gown.

    BRIDLE — Alex put the *bridle* on the horse.

11. BUT — You may go *but* come home early.

    BUTT — The goat will *butt* his head against the wall.

12. CEILING — The *ceiling* of my room is painted white.

    SEALING — Julie is *sealing* the envelopes.

13. CHORD — Play that *chord* on the piano.

    CORD — Ruben tied a *cord* around the package.

14. CREAK — The door of the haunted house will *creak*.

    CREEK — The water in the *creek* is cold.

15. COARSE — Jack bought some *coarse* sand-paper.

    COURSE — We played golf on the golf *course*. Of *course* we will come to the party.

The <u>hare</u> had pretty <u>hair</u>.

16. CAPITAL — Write your name in *capital* letters.

    CAPITOL — Our class will go to the state *capitol*.

17. FAIRY — Cinderella had a *fairy* godmother.

    FERRY — The *ferry* boat carried our car across the river.

18. FORTH — Juanita swang back and *forth*.

    FOURTH — Tom will be in *fourth* grade.

19. FOUL — Henry hit a *foul* ball.

    FOWL — A chicken is a *fowl*.

20. GROAN — We heard the ghost *groan*.

    GROWN — Pat has *grown* three inches this year.

21. HAIR — Did you cut your *hair*?

    HARE — A rabbit is sometimes called a *hare*.

22. HANGAR — Bob keeps his airplane in the *hangar*.

    HANGER — Hang your pants on the wooden *hanger*.

23. HEARD — I *heard* a cricket chirping outside.

    HERD — A *herd* of cattle ran across the field.

24. HIM — Did you see *him* swim?

    HYMN — The choir sang a *hymn* in church.

25. HOARSE — My voice is getting *hoarse*.

    HORSE — Don's *horse* is black and white.

26. KERNEL — The chicken ate a *kernel* of corn.

    COLONEL — My dad is a *colonel* in the Army.

27. KNEAD — You must *knead* the bread dough.

    NEED — How much money do you *need*?

28. KNIGHT   The *knight* wore a suit of armor.

    NIGHT   I like to look at stars at *night.*

29. LOAN   Will you *loan* me some money?

    LONE   There was a *lone* wolf in the forest.

30. MADE   Lynn *made* a paper airplane.

    MAID   The *maid* brought the tea to the queen.

31. MAIN   The governor is the *main* speaker.

    MANE   The lion's *mane* is fluffy.

32. MISSED   Leo *missed* the bus this morning.

    MIST   We could see the boat through the *mist.*

33. PANE   The baseball broke the *pane* of glass.

    PAIN   I have a *pain* in my foot.

34. PATIENCE   Our teacher has a lot of *patience.*

    PATIENTS   The *patients* are waiting for the doctor.

35. PAUSE   The speaker will *pause* when the audience laughs.

    PAWS   The dog's *paws* are muddy.

36. PEDAL   The *pedal* on my bike is broken.

    PEDDLE   The salesman will *peddle* the oranges.

37. PEER   Did you see the cat *peer* through the window?

    PIER   The boat was tied up to the *pier.*

38. POLE   The flag is high up on the *pole.*

    POLL   The students took a *poll* of the voters.

39. PRAY   The people will *pray* for rain.

    PREY   The lion ran after its *prey.*

40. PRINCIPAL   The *principal* of our school gave an award.

    PRINCIPLE   Will was the *principle* speaker at the assembly.

41. RAP   Did you *rap* on the door?

    WRAP   Cindy will *wrap* the birthday present.

42. RING   The bell will *ring* in ten minutes.
    My sister got a diamond *ring.*

    WRING   You should *wring* out your swimming suit.

43. SCENE   The artist painted a beautiful *scene.*

    SEEN   Have you *seen* my little sister?

44. SEAS   The pirates sailed on the seven *seas*.
    SEES   I think the tiger *sees* me!
    SEIZE   The police will *seize* the robber.

45. SIGHT   That sunset is a beautiful *sight*.
    SITE   We will build our cabin on that *site*.

46. SOAR   The hang–glider will *soar* into the air.
    SORE   My feet are *sore* from hiking.

47. SOME   Would you like *some* pudding?
    SUM   What is the *sum* of two plus two?

48. STAIR   The *stair* step was broken.
    STARE   Please don't *stare* at me.

49. TEA   Would you like some *tea* and cookies?
    TEE   The golfer hit the ball off the *tee*.

50. THRONE   The king sat on his *throne*.
    THROWN   Bill has *thrown* the ball farthest.

51. TIDE   The ocean *tide* knocked down the sand castle.
    TIED   The boy scout *tied* a strong knot in the rope.

52. THEIR   The players put on *their* helmets.
    THERE   Put the candy over *there*.

53. TO   Jeff is going *to* the beach.
    TOO   Sandy is going *too*.
    TWO   They have *two* dogs.

54. TOE   My big *toe* hurts.
    TOW   The *tow* truck pulled the car.

55. WAIST   Your belt fits around my *waist*.
    WASTE   Don't *waste* paper.

56. WAIT   Linda will *wait* for us after school.
    WEIGHT   Henry's *weight* is sixty–four pounds.

57. WOOD   The ladder is made of *wood*.
    WOULD   *Would* you like a popsicle?

58. WAY   Do you know the *way* to the park?
    WEIGH   How many pounds does your dog *weigh*?

59. WEAK   The sick man felt very *weak*.
    WEEK   Our vacation starts next *week*.

List 25: Level III

1. ARC — The rainbow made an *arc* in the sky.
   ARK — The *ark* sailed over the ocean.

2. ALTAR — The minister stood by the *altar* in the church.
   ALTER — The seamstress will *alter* the dress.

3. BARK — That dog has a loud *bark*.
   BARQUE — The boys sailed off in the *barque*.

4. BAD — Jeff has a *bad* cold.
   BADE — The king *bade* the prince to find the gold.

5. BARON — The *baron* owned a lot of land in the kingdom.
   BARREN — The land was *barren* because there was no rain.

6. BREAD — Do you like rye *bread?*
   BRED — The old man *bred* racing dogs.

7. BELL — The monk rang the church *bell.*
   BELLE — She is a beautiful Southern *belle.*

8. BERTH — Joe slept on the upper *berth.*
   BIRTH — The cat gave *birth* to seven kittens.

9. BOLL — The cotton *boll* is white.
   BOWL — Snoopy eats out of his dog *bowl.*

10. BORE — The movie will *bore* me.
    BOAR — The wild *boar* was shot by the hunter.

11. CACHE — The pirates found a *cache* of gold.
    CASH — We will pay *cash* for the car.

12. CAST — George has a *cast* on his broken arm.
    CASTE — Some societies have a *caste* system.

13. CEREAL — Charlie eats *cereal* for breakfast.
    SERIAL — The novels appeared in *serial* form.

14. CANNON — The soldiers shot off the *cannon.*
    CANON — The people must obey the pharaoh's *canon.*

15. CANVAS — Our tent is made of *canvas.*
    CANVASS — The scouts will *canvass* the neighborhood to sell candy.

16. CAROL — The choir sang a Christmas *carol.*
    CARREL — Juan is sitting at the study *carrel.*

The king was thrown from his throne.

17. CARAT — Lucy has a one *carat* diamond.
    CARROT — My rabbit eats a *carrot* every day.

18. CHUTE — The mail slid down the *chute.*
    SHOOT — The hunter will *shoot* the deer.

19. CUE — The actor heard his *cue* to come on stage.
    QUEUE — The people formed a *queue* along the sidewalk.

20. CURRANT — Do you like *currant* jelly?
    CURRENT — The *current* movie at the theatre is "King Kong."

21. DAYS — Our vacation will come in three *days.*
    DAZE — The man was in a *daze* after his accident.

22. DUAL — The car has *dual* controls.
    DUEL — The knights fought a *duel.*

23. FEAT — The gymnast performed a marvelous *feat.*
    FEET — My *feet* hurt!

24. FLAIR — Francis has a *flair* for drawing.
    FLARE — The policeman lit a *flare* in the dark.

25. FRIAR — The *friar* lives in a monastery.
    FRYER — That chicken is a *fryer.*

26. GATE — Close the *gate* to the pasture.
    GAIT — The old man's *gait* was very slow.

27. GILD — We will *gild* the ornaments.
    GUILD — My mother belongs to the ladies' *guild.*

28. GOURD — We grew a *gourd* in the garden.
    GORED — The bull *gored* the toreador's horse.

29. GRATE — Let's *grate* some cheese for the tacos.
    GREAT — The circus was *great!*

30. GUISE — The spy assumed the *guise* of a tourist.
    GUYS — There were three *guys* rowing the boat.

31. IDLE — The factory was *idle* during the strike.
    IDOL — The natives worshipped the *idol.*

32. LAPS — The babies sat in their mothers' *laps.*
    LAPSE — The student had a *lapse* of memory.

33. LAY — Jim *lay* down under the umbrella.
    LEI — The Hawaiians gave the tourist a *lei* of orchids.

34. LIAR   That fisherman is a terrible *liar!*

     LYRE   The musician plays the *lyre.*

35. LIE   Susy told a *lie.*

     LYE   *Lye* is a dangerous chemical.

36. LINKS   There are twenty *links* in the chain.

     LYNX   A *lynx* has killed the chickens.

37. LOOT   The robbers divided the *loot.*

     LUTE   The *lute* sounds like a guitar.

38. MAIZE   The pigs eat *maize.*

     MAZE   The rats ran around in the *maze.*

39. MALL   We went shopping at the *mall.*

     MAUL   The bear will *maul* the zebra.

40. MANNER   I don't like your *manner* of speaking.

     MANOR   The nobleman lives on a fancy *manor.*

41. MEDAL   Maria won a swimming *medal.*

     MEDDLE   Do not *meddle* in my business.

42. MINER   The *miner* was hurt in the cave-in.

     MINOR   You are a *minor* until your eighteenth birthday.

43. MIGHT   We *might* go surfing next week.

     MITE   The *mite* bit the cat.

44. MUSCLE   I strained a *muscle* in my arm.

     MUSSEL   My dad caught a *mussel* in the ocean and cooked it for dinner.

45. PROFIT   Our class made twenty dollars *profit* on the sale.

     PROPHET   The *prophet* predicted the end of the world.

46. RAISE   Do you *raise* any animals?

     RAYS   The *rays* of sunlight came through my window.

     RAZE   The bulldozer will *raze* the building.

47. READ   Al likes to *read* mystery stories.

     REED   I need a new *reed* for my clarinet.

48. SHEAR   The farmer will *shear* the sheep.

     SHEER   The wedding dress is made of *sheer* material.

49. SHOE   The athlete lost his *shoe.*

     SHOO   Please *shoo* the chickens out of the barn.

50. SOLE   The *sole* of my shoe has a hole in it.

    SOUL   I like *soul* music.

51. STRAIGHT   The arrow went *straight* to the target.

    STRAIT   The boat sailed through the *strait*.

52. SUITE   The movie stars stayed in a *suite* of rooms.

    SWEET   The fudge is very *sweet*.

53. TEAR   The child shed a *tear* for her lost puppy.

    TIER   We sat on the third *tier* of the auditorium.

54. TENSE   Chad was very *tense* during the spelling bee.

    TENTS   The scouts pitched their *tents*.

55. VANE   The weather *vane* indicated a storm was coming.

    VEIN   The *vein* on my hand looks blue.

    VAIN   The queen is *vain* about her appearance.

56. WAIVE   The coach will *waive* the requirement.

    WAVE   The surfer came in on a big *wave*.

              Did you *wave* to your mother?

List 26: Homographs

OBJECTIVE

To develop the student's ability to understand the different meanings of homograph pairs and to use the words appropriately in functional language.

Buck/buck

APPLICATIONS

See activities under List 25, Homophones.

ACT	Jack will *act* in the play. He is in the second *act* of the play.
BACK	My *back* hurts. My kitty came *back* home.
BALL	Cinderella went to the *ball*. Bill bounced the *ball* against the wall.
BANGS	The firecrackers make loud *bangs*. Jennie has short *bangs* on her forehead.
BANK	The river overflowed its *bank*. Jacob has fifty dollars in the *bank*.
BARK	The collie has a loud *bark*. The *bark* of the tree peels off.
BAT	My baseball *bat* is broken. The *bat* flew out of the cave.
BED	My *bed* is very soft. We planted a *bed* of roses.
BILL	Will you pay the *bill?* The bird carried a worm in her *bill*.
BIT	The tiger *bit* the giraffe. My finger hurts a little *bit*.
BLOCK	The puppy ran around the *block*. The football player will *block* the runner.
BLUE	I feel very *blue* today. Barbie has a *blue* dress.
BOW	Please *bow* to the audience. The *bow* of the ship was out of the wate
BOX	Put your games in the *box*. The prizefighters will *box* tonight.
BRIGHT	The moon is *bright* tonight. The college student is very *bright*.
BULB	Josie planted the daffodil *bulb*. ʼightbulb is burned out.

53

CAN

An aluminum *can* may be recycled.
Can you draw an elephant?

CHANGE

I have fifty cents in *change*.
Would you like to *change* your name?

CHARGE

My mom will *charge* the clothes at the store.
How much do you *charge* for piano lessons?

CHECK

The bank gave me a *check*.
Will you *check* on the babies?

CHEST

The pirate opened the treasure *chest*.
The gorilla pounded on his *chest*.

COAT

Alice has a new fur *coat*.
Dad put a *coat* of paint on the kitchen wall.

CROW

The black *crow* flew over the cornfield.
The rooster will *crow* in the morning.

DATE

Would you like to eat a *date* or a prune?
My sister went on a *date* with her boyfriend.

DECK

The sailors stood on the *deck* of the ship.
Do you have a *deck* of cards?

DRAW

The cowboy will *draw* his gun.
The artist will *draw* a picture.

DUCK

Duck your head when you crawl in the cave.
The little *duck* said "quack."

DULL

This knife is very *dull*.
The play is *dull* and boring.

EAR

I can hear with my *ear*.
Sally ate an *ear* of corn.

FACE

Your *face* is sunburned.
Please *face* the audience.

FAINT

Did you ever *faint*?
We heard a *faint* noise in the distance.

FAIR

The State *Fair* is in October.
The weather will be *fair* and warm.

FALL

We have football games in the *fall*.
The leaves *fall* off the trees.

FELT

The doll is made of *felt*.
The prisoner *felt* sorry.

FILE

The secretary will *file* the papers.
Do you *file* your fingernails?

FINE

Jeff paid a *fine* for speeding.
I feel just *fine*.

FIT

The child had a *fit* because she wanted the candy.
My new cowboy hat doesn't *fit*.

FLY

That *fly* is bothering me.
Dave hit a pop *fly* in the baseball game.

FOOL

Gail tried to *fool* me on April Fool's Day.
The *fool* did tricks before the king.

FOOT	The baby is one *foot* tall. My *foot* won't fit in that shoe.
GOBBLE	The pig will *gobble* his food very fast. The turkey says "*gobble,* gobble."
GROUND	The *ground* is covered with snow. Mother *ground* up the meat for meatloaf.
HAND	Pat broke her *hand.* The audience gave the actor a *hand.*
HANG	*Hang* the picture on that wall. The boys *hang* around the school on Sundays.
HARD	The test was so *hard.* The clay will get *hard* overnight.
HEAD	Manuel is at the *head* of the class. I put a ski cap on my *head.*
HIDE	Do you *hide* Easter eggs? The elephant's *hide* is very tough.
HIT	The song was a big *hit.* Danny *hit* the ball into left field.
ICE	Sarah will *ice* the cake. Don't walk on thin *ice.*
IRON	Rebecca will *iron* her skirt. The gate is made of *iron.*
JAM	Do you like cherry *jam?* The crowd will *jam* into the room.
JOKER	Tony is a practical *joker.* Is the *joker* in that deck of cards?
KEY	The piano *key* is broken. Do you have your house *key?*
KID	We have a new *kid* in our class. A *kid* is a baby goat.
KIND	Rudy is *kind* to animals. What *kind* of ice cream is that?
LAND	The jet will *land* at the airport. The pilgrims came to a new *land.*
LAST	The cartoon did not *last* long. Leroy bought the *last* comic book at the store.
LEAVES	The colorful *leaves* fell off the trees. Becky *leaves* for school at eight o'clock.
LEFT	I write with my *left* hand. Jill *left* the movie theater.
LETTER	Pearl got a *letter* in the mail. Print the first *letter* of your name.
LIE	Don't ever tell a *lie.* The tiger will *lie* down after his dinner.
LIGHT	Is that box *light* or heavy? Turn on the *light.*

Homographs (continued)

LIKE
Do you *like* popsicles?
Frances looks *like* Lynn.

LINE
Sara was first in *line*.
Tony drew a long *line* on his paper.

MATCH
Eddie was in the wrestling *match*.
Hans lit a *match* in the dark.

MEAN
What do you *mean*?
The lion is very *mean*.

MIGHT
Juan *might* go fishing Saturday.
Paul Bunyan swung the ax with all his *might*.

MINE
The boys worked in the gold *mine*.
This piece of cake is *mine*.

MISS
Do you *miss* your sister?
The dart might *miss* the target.

NAIL
The *nail* on my thumb broke.
Hit the *nail* with your hammer.

NOTE
Can you play this *note* on your trumpet?
Anita wrote a *note* to her friend.

PARK
Our team plays baseball at the *park*.
We'll *park* our car by the tent.

PART
I *part* my hair in the middle.
John gave me *part* of his candy bar.

PASS
Hannah will *pass* to the fourth grade.
Miguel threw a *pass* to Martin.

PEEP
The little chick can *peep* very loud.
The child will *peep* through the window.

PEN
The pigs live in a *pen*.
My *pen* ran out of ink.

PET
A beagle makes a nice *pet*.
Are you afraid to *pet* that horse?

PIPE
My dad smokes a *pipe*.
The water *pipe* burst.

PITCHER
Martha is the *pitcher* on our team.
Lucy poured lemonade out of her *pitcher*.

PLAY
Amy will be Raggedy Ann in the *play*.
Can you *play* basketball with me?

POINT
Please don't *point* at people.
My pencil has a sharp *point*.

POOL
Lupe has a *pool* table at her house.
Let's go to the swimming *pool*.

POP
What kind of *pop* do you drink?
Alex will *pop* the balloon.

POUND
I'd like a *pound* of chocolates.
We bought our dog at the dog *pound*.

PUNCH
Connie likes to drink *punch* for lunch.
We can *punch* this punching bag.

RARE
  I like to eat *rare* steak.
  Diamonds are *rare* jewels.

RECORD
  I bought a new *record* album yesterday.
  Paul set a track *record* in the Olympics.

REST
  I like to *rest* after dinner.
  You may have the *rest* of the ice cream.

RIGHT
  I wear my watch on my *right* hand.
  You got every answer *right!*

ROCK
  My grandma likes to *rock* in her chair.
  We found a beautiful *rock* in the mountains.

ROLL
  The ball will *roll* down the hill.
  I ate a *roll* with my dinner.

ROSE
  The *rose* smells very nice.
  The crowd *rose* to greet the President.

RULER
  The king is the *ruler* of his country.
  Measure the cloth with your *ruler.*

RUN
  Pete will *run* five miles.
  Helen got a *run* in her stocking.

SCALES
  The fish is covered with *scales.*
  I weighed myself on the *scales.*

SCREEN
  Please set up the movie *screen.*
  The *screen* door slammed.

SEAL
  The *seal* balanced a ball on his nose.
  Seal the envelope, please.

SET
  Our television *set* is broken.
  Paula *set* the table for dinner.

SHED
  The spaniel will *shed* his fur in the summer.
  Adam put the tools in the *shed.*

SHEET
  Lynn bought a pretty *sheet* for her bed.
  Hand me a *sheet* of paper.

SHINE
  Did you *shine* your shoes?
  Shine your flashlight over here.

SHOCK
  Aaron got a *shock* from the electric wire.
  That movie will *shock* my dad.

SINK
  The *sink* is leaking.
  I hope our boat will not *sink* in the lake.

SKIP
  Do you know how to *skip?*
  We will *skip* the next problem.

SOCK
  Joe lost his *sock* at the park.
  Julius might *sock* Bill on the chin.

SPACE
  The rocket blasted off into *space.*
  Write your name in that *space.*

SPEAKER
  The governor was the *speaker* at the celebration.
  The stereo has a big *speaker.*

SPRING
  Spring is my favorite season.
  Joe's car has a broken *spring.*

SQUASH   Do you like to eat *squash?*
The dog will *squash* the plant.

STAND   Jack and Jill have a lemonade *stand.*
Stand up when you salute the flag.

STICK   The stamp will not *stick* to the letter.
Vic broke the *stick* in two pieces.

TABLET   The doctor told me to eat this cold *tablet.*
I have written on every page of my *tablet.*

TAG   Let's play *tag* on the lawn.
Did you put a name *tag* on your suitcase?

TIP   Tony left a *tip* for the waiter.
I cut the *tip* of my finger.

TOP   The *top* is spinning fast.
Write your name at the *top* of the page.

TRAIN   Hank will *train* his dog to do tricks.
Kim likes to ride the *train.*

TRIP   Will you take a *trip* this summer?
Julius might *trip* over that chair in the dark.

WATCH   Michele got a *watch* for Christmas.
Did you *watch* that movie?

WAVE   The *wave* was good for surfing.
Al will *wave* to his grandpa.

WELL   Frances plays the piano *well.*
The cat fell into the *well.*

Advanced Homographs

ARMS   My *arms* and legs hurt.
The soldiers laid down their *arms.*

BASE   The *base* of the statue broke.
Carl ran to third *base.*

BEAR   The grizzly *bear* is dangerous.
I can't *bear* to be alone.

BLOW   Can you *blow* up this balloon?
The boxer gave him a *blow* on the head.

BLUFF   I had to *bluff* on the exam.
The Indian stood on the *bluff.*

BRAND   The cowboy put a *brand* on his horse.
What *brand* is that corn?

BUCK   I paid one *buck* for that toy.
The horse may *buck* you off.

CALF   A *calf* is a baby cow.
The *calf* of my leg hurts.

CAST   The *cast* of the play had a party.
Bill has a *cast* on his broken arm.

CORN   We ate *corn* on the cob.
I have a *corn* on my toe.

COURT   The judge came into the *court*.
               The prince wanted to *court* Cinderella.

DART   Henry threw the *dart* at the dartboard.
               Betsy sewed a *dart* in her dress.

DOWN   The duck has very soft *down* on his back.
               Come *down* the ladder carefully.

FAST   The race cars go very *fast*.
               We don't eat food on a *fast* day.

FIRM   My dad works in a law *firm*.
               I sleep on a *firm* mattress.

FLEET   The *fleet* of ships is in the harbor.
               The runner was *fleet* of foot.

FLOAT   The astronauts can *float* in space.
               We made a *float* for the parade.

GAME   Monopoly is my favorite *game*.
               The men went *game* hunting.

HOLD   Ruben got to *hold* the monkey.
               The pirates put the money in the ship's *hold*.

JAR   Put the bugs in the *jar*.
               Did the crash *jar* the wheel loose?

JUMPER   Patsy wore a plaid *jumper* to school.
               Bill is a good *jumper*.

LAP   My poodle can *lap* up milk fast.
               Judy's cat sits on her *lap*.

LEAN   Jack Sprat ate *lean* meat.
               Don't *lean* against that wall.

LOAF   The *loaf* of bread smells delicious.
               The hobo will *loaf* all day.

LOG   Lupe kept a daily *log* of her travels.
               We put the *log* in the fireplace.

LONG   I *long* to see my grandmother.
               The movie "King Kong" is very *long*.

MOLD   There was *mold* on the bread.
               Pour the wax into the *mold*.

NAP   Connie took a *nap* in the hammock.
               There is a lot of *nap* on that blanket.

PAGE   What *page* is that story on?
               The *page* knelt before the king.

PALM   Arizona has a lot of *palm* trees.
               I cut the *palm* of my hand.

PERCH   The parakeet sat on his *perch*.
               There are lots of *perch* in the ocean.

PICK   You may *pick* out some candy.
               The miner uses a *pick* and shovel.

PIT   A peach has a large *pit* inside.
               We saw some rattlesnakes in the deep *pit*.

PLANE
Joe flew the *plane* over the school.
The carpenter will *plane* the wood until it is smooth.

PUPIL
Ruby is the best *pupil* in the class.
The *pupil* in your eye is black.

QUACK
The duck will *quack* when he sees you.
The *quack* pretended he was a doctor.

RACE
Let's run a *race!*
What *race* of people do you belong to?

RACKET
Carmen has a new tennis *racket.*
The animals make a loud *racket* at the zoo.

RANGE
The cowboy rides his horse on the *range.*
Ernest is cooking on his new *range.*

REAR
The horse may *rear* if he is scared.
We stood in the *rear* of the theater.

ROUND
Mary has a *round* face.
The boxer got hurt in the sixth *round* of the fight.

RUNG
John has *rung* the bell three times.
A *rung* of the ladder is broken.

SHIFT
Pete's dad works on the night *shift* at the factory.
The car must *shift* gears to go uphill.

SOIL
Plant the flower in good *soil.*
The paint might *soil* your shirt.

SPOKE
The *spoke* on the bicycle is broken.
Ernest *spoke* to the President.

SPRAY
Anita will *spray* the lawn.
That *spray* of flowers is beautiful.

STALL
The horse is in his *stall.*
My car might *stall* at the stop light.

STEER
Can you *steer* your bicycle?
The cowboy roped the *steer.*

STORY
Our apartment is on the second *story.*
Miguel told the first graders a *story.*

STRIKE
Did you *strike* out in the baseball game?
The workers are on *strike.*

STUMP
Helen sat on the tree *stump.*
That question will *stump* the panel.

SWALLOW
The pretty *swallow* flew up to the tree.
My throat hurts when I *swallow.*

YARD
Darcy has a rabbit in her *yard.*
Mandy bought a *yard* of material for her dress.

List 27: Heteronyms

OBJECTIVE

To develop the student's ability to understand the different meanings of heteronym pairs and use the words in meaningful language.

APPLICATIONS

The girl with a bōw took a bow.

- Talk about accents in words and how they can change the meanings. Also discuss deriving meanings of words from sentence context. Introduce heteronym pairs.

- Make up additional sentences for each pair. Present a sentence orally and omit the heteronym but show it on a card. The student must say the correct form of the word to complete the sentence.

- Have students make up sentences using both words in a heteronym pair (see illustration).

1. ADDRESS — My ad´-dress is 134 State Street.
   The governor will ad-dress´ the students.

2. BOW — Susie wears a bow (bō) in her hair.
   The actor will bow (bou) to the audience.

3. CLOSE — Please close (clōz) the door.
   The cat is sitting close (clōs) to the dog.

4. CONTENT — What was the con´-tent of his speech?
   I am con-tent´ to stay home and watch TV.

5. CONTRAST — Will you con-trast´ a watermelon and a cantaloupe?
   There is a great con´-trast between Republicans and Democrats.

6. CONVERT — Louise is a con´-vert from jogging to tennis.
   We will con-vert´ our van to a camper.

7. CONVICT — The con´-vict escaped from the prison.
   Will the jury con-vict´ that woman?

8. DIGEST — You will di-gest´ your food in eight hours.
   Do you read the *Reader's Di´-gest?*

9. DOVE — Bill dove (dōv) into the water.
   The dove (dŭv) makes a cooing noise.

10. INVALID — The in´-va-lid is in the hospital.
    Mary's driver's license is in-val´-id.

11. LEAD — The drum major will lead (lēd) the parade.
    The lead (lĕd) weight is very heavy.

12. LIVE — Where do you live (lĭv)?
    We caught a live (līv) bird.

13. MINUTE — I can hold my breath for one min´-ute.
    The bug has min-ute´ legs.

14. OBJECT   Larry bought me an ob'-ject of great value.
                                Does your mother ob-ject' to your playing tennis?

15. PRESENT   I got a big pres'-ent for Christmas.
                                The coach will pre-sent' the awards.

16. PROJECT   Are you finished with your science proj'-ect?
                                Pro-ject' the film on the screen.

17. READ   Henry likes to read (rēd) comic books.
                                My dad read (rĕd) a ghost story to us.

18. RECORD   Let's re-cord' our radio play.
                                Julie bought a new rec'-ord for her stereo.

19. ROW   The bunnies were lined up in a row (rō).
                                The neighbors had a row (rou) over ownership of the fence.

20. SOW   The farmer will sow (sō) the wheat.
                                The old sow (sou) is in the pigpen.

21. SUBJECT   What is the sub'-ject of your talk?
                                The enemy may sub-ject' the prisoners to torture.

22. TEAR   Nancy shed a tear (tēr) for her lost puppy.
                                Don't tear (târ) up your paper.

23. WIND   You should wind (wīnd) up your watch each morning.
                                The wind (wĭnd) blew down the palm tree.

24. WOUND   The doctor put a bandage on the wound (wōōnd).
                                Nick wound (wound) the string around his yoyo.

Lists 28–30: Antonyms

OBJECTIVE

To develop the student's ability to identify, understand and use opposite words.

APPLICATIONS

modern   *antique*

* Discuss the meanings of antonym pairs. Think of synonyms for the words.

* Write the antonyms on two sets of cards. The students find the matching pairs and make sentences for the words.

* Present a sentence orally using one of the words. The student replaces the word with its antonym as he repeats the sentence.

    Example: The vase is *old.*
    The vase is *new.*

* Write the antonym pairs on cards. Two students <u>act out</u> the two words and other students guess the antonyms (happy — sad).

* Students use both words in one sentence to illustrate the meanings.

    Example: Wheat is *abundant* but water is *scarce.*
    Paul is *generous* but his sister is *stingy.*

* Play antonym baseball. The student gets one point for each antonym he can name when its opposite is "pitched" to him. He must also use it in a sentence.

* Make lists on 5 x 7 cards for students to match antonym pairs. Students draw lines to connect the words. Laminate the cards for learning center use.

* Refer to List 62, Antonym Analogies.

List 28: Level I

1.	after	before	20.	dead	alive
2.	all	none	21.	dirty	clean
3.	always	never	22.	early	late
4.	asleep	awake	23.	easy	hard
5.	beautiful	ugly	24.	empty	full
6.	before	after	25.	fat	skinny
7.	behind	in front	26.	find	lose
8.	below	above	27.	front	back
9.	best	worst	28.	happy	sad
10.	black	white	29.	hard	soft
11.	boy	girl	30.	healthy	sick
12.	brother	sister	31.	heavy	light
13.	city	country	32.	high	low
14.	closed	open	33.	husband	wife
15.	cold	hot	34.	kind	mean
16.	come	go	35.	king	queen
17.	dark	light	36.	last	first
18.	daughter	son	37.	laugh	cry
19.	day	night	38.	left	right

Antonyms (continued)

39.	little	big		54.	she	he
40.	long	short		55.	sick	well
41.	lock	unlock		56.	slow	fast
42.	man	woman		57.	small	large
43.	morning	night		58.	smart	dumb
44.	mother	father		59.	take	give
45.	near	far		60.	top	bottom
46.	new	old		61.	ugly	pretty
47.	noisy	quiet		62.	under	over
48.	off	on		63.	up	down
49.	old	new		64.	wet	dry
50.	out	in		65.	work	play
51.	poor	rich		66.	yes	no
52.	push	pull		67.	young	old
53.	right	wrong				

List 29: Level II

1.	absent	present		34.	length	width
2.	against	for		35.	loose	tight
3.	beneath	above		36.	lose	find
4.	bitter	sweet		37.	lower	raise
5.	borrow	lend		38.	often	seldom
6.	brave	scared		39.	outer	inner
7.	buy	sell		40.	part	whole
8.	careful	careless		41.	patient	impatient
9.	cheerful	sad		42.	polite	rude
10.	complete	incomplete		43.	quick	slow
11.	cruel	kind		44.	question	answer
12.	crooked	straight		45.	reward	punishment
13.	death	life		46.	rough	smooth
14.	deep	shallow		47.	sell	buy
15.	different	same		48.	send	receive
16.	double	single		49.	selfish	unselfish
17.	east	west		50.	sharp	dull
18.	enemy	friend		51.	sink	float
19.	exciting	dull		52.	south	north
20.	exit	entrance		53.	stay	go
21.	expensive	cheap		54.	stranger	friend
22.	fancy	plain		55.	strong	weak
23.	finish	begin		56.	sweet	sour
24.	floor	ceiling		57.	tame	wild
25.	foolish	wise		58.	thick	thin
26.	forget	remember		59.	true	false
27.	forward	backward		60.	uncertain	certain
28.	graceful	clumsy		61.	wake	sleep
29.	guilty	innocent		62.	war	peace
30.	hide	show		63.	warm	cool
31.	increase	decrease		64.	whisper	yell
32.	intelligent	stupid		65.	wide	narrow
33.	lead	follow		66.	winter	summer

List 30: Level III

1.	abundant	scarce	47.	joy	grief
2.	accept	refuse	48.	knowledge	ignorance
3.	accidental	intentional	49.	lazy	industrious
4.	accurate	incorrect	50.	literal	figurative
5.	admit	deny	51.	majority	minority
6.	advance	retreat	52.	maximum	minimum
7.	antique	modern	53.	merciful	cruel
8.	attack	defend	54.	miserable	happy
9.	authentic	imitation	55.	mix	sort
10.	beg	offer	56.	moist	dry
11.	cease	begin	57.	naked	clothed
12.	combine	separate	58.	necessary	useless
13.	comedy	tragedy	59.	nourish	starve
14.	condemn	praise	60.	obey	disobey
15.	conquer	fail	61.	perfect	faulty
16.	contract	expand	62.	permit	forbid
17.	dangerous	safe	63.	positive	negative
18.	depart	arrive	64.	private	public
19.	destroy	create	65.	prohibit	allow
20.	discourage	encourage	66.	reluctant	enthusiastic
21.	disgrace	honor	67.	sane	insane
22.	drunk	sober	68.	simple	complicated
23.	dwarf	giant	69.	shrink	expand
24.	evil	good	70.	slavery	freedom
25.	exhibit	conceal	71.	solid	liquid
26.	exterior	interior	72.	spend	save
27.	extinguish	ignite	73.	stationary	movable
28.	fail	succeed	74.	stiff	limp
29.	famous	unknown	75.	strengthen	weaken
30.	fertile	barren	76.	swift	slow
31.	fiction	fact	77.	tardy	early
32.	former	latter	78.	temporary	permanent
33.	frequent	infrequent	79.	thaw	freeze
34.	gather	scatter	80.	tough	tender
35.	genuine	fake	81.	triumph	fail
36.	generous	stingy	82.	unbreakable	fragile
37.	grin	frown	83.	unique	ordinary
38.	harmony	discord	84.	useful	useless
39.	harsh	mild	85.	usually	rarely
40.	idle	busy	86.	vacant	occupied
41.	imaginary	real	87.	vanish	appear
42.	import	export	88.	victory	defeat
43.	imprison	free	89.	villain	hero
44.	illegal	lawful	90.	violent	gentle
45.	include	exclude	91.	wealth	poverty
46.	interior	superior	92.	worthless	valuable

List 31: Adjectives

plain

sweet

sour

hot

OBJECTIVE

To develop the student's ability to understand the meanings of adjectives and use them for precision of meaning in functional language.

APPLICATIONS

♦ Give students one list of words such as SIZE. Have them order the words in sequence.

> Example: wee — tiny — small — middle-sized — big — huge — giant

They can also draw a picture for each word.

♦ *Adjective Game*
Make one set of twenty cards with pictures of people, animals or objects on them (cut pictures from old workbooks or use stickers). Make a second set with adjectives printed on them. Lay out cards in Set 1 face-up on the table. The student draws a card from Set 2 and finds a picture it describes. He uses the words in a sentence and covers the picture.

> Example: The *black cat* ate his food.

♦ Bring in an interesting object. The students brainstorm adjectives to describe it. List the words on a chart and let students add to it during the day.

Example: FISHBOWL		
shiny	glass	clear
open	wet	breakable
round	hard	middle-sized
solid	smooth	transparent
heavy	fragile	

Have students write or tell a short story about the object using many of these words.

♦ Select one adjective. Have students think of all the words it could describe.

Example: STRAIGHT		
arrow	yardstick	hair
line	pole	edge

♦ Refer to List 84, Emotions and Feelings, for more adjectives to act out.

Size

average	miniature	petite	wee
big	great	puny	little
colossal	giant	small	immense
fat	huge	short	massive
gigantic	long	tiny	middle-sized
mammoth	large	tall	

Quantity

abundant	few	heavy	many
empty	light	numerous	

Shape

broad	hollow	round	shallow
chubby	low	square	skinny
deep	narrow	straight	wide
flat	crooked	steep	curved
high			

Time

brief	old	young	ancient
early	quick	rapid	modern
fast	slow	long	old-fashioned
late	swift	short	

Sound

hushed	quiet	soft	purring
hissing	silent	squealing	resonant
harsh	shrill	booming	cooing
loud	thundering	crying	deafening
mute	voiceless	screaming	high-pitched
moaning	faint	whispering	raspy
noisy	screeching	husky	melodic

Taste and Smell

bitter	ripe	sticky	sour
delicious	rotten	thirsty	spicy
fresh	sweet	tasty	strong
juicy	stale	salty	tasteless

Touch

bumpy	dry	icy	silky
broken	damaged	loose	slimy
breezy	dusty	plastic	solid
boiling	fuzzy	prickly	steady
cool	filthy	rainy	slushy
curly	fluttering	rough	shaky
chilly	fluffy	shaggy	tender
crooked	flaky	smooth	tight
cuddly	grubby	sticky	wooden
cold	greasy	shivering	weak
creepy	melted	scattered	wet
dirty	hot	sharp	uneven
damp	hard	soft	slippery

Appearance

adorable	cloudy	motionless	shiny
alert	crowded	muddy	sparkling
bright	clean	glamorous	stormy
blonde	dark	graceful	smoggy
bloody	dull	grotesque	strange
clear	distinct	gleaming	spotless
colorful	elegant	homely	ugly
cute	fancy	light	unsightly
beautiful	filthy	poised	unusual
blushing	misty	quaint	

Adjectives (continued)

Feelings (positive)

good	exuberant	hilarious	relieved
amused	elated	happy	silly
agreeable	enthusiastic	healthy	successful
brave	eager	joyous	smiling
comfortable	excited	jolly	splendid
courageous	faithful	kind	victorious
calm	friendly	lovely	vivacious
cooperative	funny	lucky	witty
cheerful	fair	lively	zealous
charming	fine	obedient	
determined	gentle	pleasant	
enchanting	glorious	perfect	

Feelings (negative)

afraid	defiant	homeless	selfish
angry	dangerous	ill	troubled
anxious	eerie	lonely	tense
annoyed	embarrassed	mysterious	thoughtless
awful	envious	naughty	tired
ashamed	evil	nervous	upset
bad	frightened	outrageous	uptight
bored	fierce	obnoxious	worried
creepy	frantic	panicky	wicked
cruel	foolish	repulsive	weary
defeated	grieving	sore	
disgusting	hungry	scornful	
depressed	hurt	scary	

Condition

alive	dead	innocent	rich
brainy	doubtful	impossible	super
breakable	difficult	important	shy
busy	different	modern	sleepy
careful	easy	open	tame
curious	famous	outstanding	uninterested
crazy	fragile	puzzled	wrong
concerned	helpful	powerful	wild
cautious	helpless	poor	wandering
clever	inquisitive	real	

Lists 32–33: Adverbs

OBJECTIVE

To develop the student's ability to understand the meanings of adverbs and use the words appropriately in his language.

gently
hastily
happily
cautiously
promptly

APPLICATIONS

♦ Talk about the meanings of adverbs. Demonstrate by using body movements if possible.

♦ Make a set of twenty cards with pictures of actions being performed (cut out pictures from old workbooks or use stickers). Make a second set with adverbs printed on them. Lay out cards in Set 1 face-up on the table. The student draws a card from Set 2 and finds a picture it describes. He uses the words in a sentence and covers the picture.

    Example: The boy *hit the ball quickly.*

♦ Have the student cut out pictures from magazines. He should find an adverb that describes a picture, paste the picture into a mini-book and write a sentence below the picture using the adverb.

    Example: The boy is running *fast.*

♦ *Acting Adverbs*

For each sentence on List 33, make a chart listing the words in parentheses. Read the first part of the sentence. One student acts out the sentence using one adverb he selects from the corresponding chart. The others guess which adverb he has chosen. A second student may act out the same sentence with a different adverb and so on. This activity should help the students see the subtle differences in word meaning.

New sentences can be created to go with the adverb groups to extend the activity. Students' names may be substituted in the sentences.

List 32: Adverbs

accidentally	calmly	enormously	gladly
afterwards	carefully	enthusiastically	gracefully
almost	carelessly	equally	greedily
always	cautiously	even	happily
angrily	cheerfully	eventually	hastily
annually	clearly	exactly	honestly
anxiously	correctly	faithfully	hourly
awkwardly	courageously	far	hungrily
badly	crossly	fast	innocently
blindly	cruelly	fatally	inquisitively
boldly	daily	fiercely	irritably
boastfully	defiantly	fondly	joyously
bravely	deliberately	foolishly	justly
briefly	doubtfully	fortunately	kindly
brightly	easily	frantically	lazily
busily	elegantly	gently	less

Adverbs (continued)

loosely	politely	selfishly	swiftly
loudly	poorly	seriously	tenderly
madly	powerfully	shakily	tensely
merrily	promptly	sharply	thoughtfully
monthly	punctually	shrilly	tightly
more	quickly	shyly	too
mortally	quietly	silently	tomorrow
mysteriously	rapidly	sleepily	truthfully
nearly	rarely	slowly	unexpectedly
neatly	really	smoothly	very
nervously	recklessly	softly	victoriously
never	regularly	solemnly	violently
noisily	reluctantly	sometimes	vivaciously
not	repeatedly	soon	warmly
obediently	rightfully	speedily	weakly
obnoxiously	roughly	stealthily	wearily
often	rudely	sternly	well
only	sadly	successfully	wildly
painfully	safely	suddenly	yearly
perfectly	seldom	suspiciously	yesterday

List 33: Acting Adverbs

1. Judy called her friend — (politely — clearly — continuously — sleepily — quickly)
2. Sam walked into the room — (awkwardly — suspiciously — blindly — lazily — quietly)
3. John picked up the cat — (gently — hastily — happily — cautiously — promptly)
4. Alan cut the wood — (busily — exactly — sadly — accidentally — fiercely)
5. José divided his money — (greedily — equally — calmly — quickly — silently)
6. Susan left the party — (punctually — angrily — briefly — suddenly — frantically)
7. Cindy ate the candy bar — (selfishly — innocently — noisily — shakily — hungrily)
8. Abner picked up the weights — (painfully — successfully — anxiously — enthusiastically — seriously)
9. Lucy modeled the dress — (elegantly — obediently — cheerfully — nervously — wearily)
10. Chris recited the rhyme — (shrilly — faintly — shyly — tensely — quickly)
11. Louise tied the knot — (speedily — tightly — wildly — cleverly — repeatedly)
12. Kim threw the ball — (carelessly — slowly — rapidly — victoriously — often)
13. T. J. played cards — (mysteriously — boastfully — carefully — cheerfully — fast)
14. Charlie put on the costume — (neatly — irritably — quickly — sadly — thoughtfully)
15. Kevin ran down the stairs — (often — smoothly — silently — vivaciously — noisily)
16. Michele swam across the pool — (wildly — victoriously — smoothly — sadly — painfully)
17. Anita told the story — (honestly — joyously — lazily — calmly — loudly)
18. Frank went into the haunted house (stealthily — suddenly — defiantly — blindly — anxiously)
19. Don broke the toy — (accidentally — boldly — deliberately — noisily — quietly)
20. Phyllis drew the picture — (tightly — vivaciously — swiftly — shakily — seriously)

List 34: Abbreviations

OBJECTIVE

To develop the student's ability to identify, understand and use correct abbreviated forms.

APPLICATIONS

A.M.   P.M.

- After discussing the meanings of the abbreviations, let the students "decode" some secret messages.

    Example: The *Dr.* bought two *lbs.* of meat and three *ft.* of rope on *Thurs., Apr.* 20.

- Let students make up sentences for others to decode.

- Make one set of cards with abbreviations and matching words on another set to be paired by students.

- Student draws two abbreviation cards and makes up a sentence using the two words.

Time		Measurement	
Mon.	Monday	a.	amp
Tues.	Tuesday	v.	volt
Wed.	Wednesday	cm.	centimeter
Thurs.	Thursday	g.	gram
Fri.	Friday	km.	kilometer
Sat.	Saturday	kg.	kilogram
Sun.	Sunday	m.	meter
Jan.	January	mm.	millimeter
Feb.	February	c.	cup
Mar.	March	tsp. or t.	teaspoon
Apr.	April	tbsp. or T.	tablespoon
Aug.	August	lb. (#)	pound
Sept.	September	oz.	ounce
Oct.	October	dz.	dozen
Nov.	November	gal.	gallon
Dec.	December	pt.	pint
A.M.	midnight to noon	qt.	quart
P.M.	noon to midnight	bu.	bushel
B.C.	Before Christ	in. ('')	inch
A.D.	Anno Domini (year of our Lord)	ft. (')	foot
		yd.	yard
hr.	hour	mi.	mile
min.	minute	ht.	height
mo.	month	wt.	weight
sec.	second	hp.	horsepower
yr.	year	mph.	miles per hour
wk.	week	no. (#)	number
		sq.	square
		pct. (%)	percent

Abbreviations (continued)

Place

Ave.	avenue
Blvd.	boulevard
Ct.	court
Co.	county
Hwy.	highway
Pl.	place
Rd.	road
St.	street
Sq.	square
D.C.	District of Columbia
H.S.	High School
P.O.	Post Office
R.R.	Railroad
U.S.A.	United States of America

Titles

Capt.	Captain
Dr.	Doctor
Gov.	Governor
Gen.	General
Hon.	Honorable
Jr.	Junior
Lt.	Lieutenant
Pres.	President
Rev.	Reverend
St.	Saint
Sr.	Senior
Sgt.	Sergeant
ref.	referee
mgr.	manager

Miscellaneous

bldg.	building
C.O.D.	Collect on Delivery
etc.	and so forth
P.S.	Post Script
ch.	chapter
p.	page
©	copyright
R.S.V.P.	please reply (French)

List 35: Similes

OBJECTIVE

To develop the student's ability to understand the meanings of common similes which will expand and enrich his language comprehension.

APPLICATIONS

Hairy as an ape.

* Print the similes on cards. The student draws a card and must use the simile in a logical sentence.

    Example: The house is *neat as a pin*.

* Help students think of other appropriate words that could be substituted for the last word.

    Example: black as coal
    black as tar
    black as night
    black as a crow
    black as a panther

* Refer to List 31, Adjectives. Students can make up new similes with these words.

    Example: defiant as a jaguar

* Find magazine pictures to go with the similes. Paste into a mini–book and label.

Animals

sly/cunning as a fox
wise as an owl
fat as a pig
quiet as a mouse
strong as an ox
huge as an elephant
proud as a peacock
playful as a kitten
sick as a dog
gentle as a lamb
mad as a March hare
hairy as an ape
clumsy as an ox
poor as a churchmouse

slow as a snail
happy as a lark
busy as a bee
slippery as an eel
brave as a lion
snug as a bug
quick as a cat
cross as a bear
blind as a bat
free as a bird
hungry as a wolf
nervous as a cat
mad as a hornet
obstinate/stubborn
    as a mule

Color

green as grass
white as snow
white as a ghost
white as a sheet

black as coal
black as ink
red as a beet
blue as the sky

Other

warm as toast
tough as nails
cool as a cucumber
deep as the ocean
limp as a dishrag
pretty as a picture
thin as a rail
smart as a whip
neat as a pin
quick as a wink
hard as a rock
clear as crystal/a bell
dead as a doornail
sharp as a tack/razor
dry as a bone
straight as an arrow
old as the hills
ugly as sin

good as gold
heavy as a lead weight
smooth as satin/velvet
cold as ice
wicked as a witch
high as a kite
stiff as a board
slow as molasses in
    January
flat as a pancake
sweet as sugar
regular as clockwork
tough as leather
pleased as punch
light as a feather
fresh as a daisy
fit as a fiddle

Lists 36-39: Idioms

In one ear and out the other.

OBJECTIVE

To develop the student's ability to understand the meanings of common idioms so as to expand his comprehension of language.

APPLICATIONS

◆ Let students use context clues and guess the meanings of idioms after you use them in sentences. Then discuss them.

◆ Have students listen for idioms at home for a week. They should bring in lists of all the idioms they hear. Students then explain the idioms on their lists to others in the group.

◆ Select some idioms for students to illustrate literal and figurative meanings.

List 36: Food and Colors

Food
she's a peach
full of beans
not my cup of tea
full of baloney
sour grapes
that's corny
in a pickle
bring home the bacon
in a stew
top banana
salt of the earth
worth his salt
peas in a pod
nuts about you
piece of cake
can't have cake and eat it too
he's a real ham
hard nut to crack
let's talk turkey
a bad egg
break the ice
baker's dozen
finger in every pie
pot luck
hard boiled
apple of my eye
rotten egg

Colors
in the pink
in the red
feeling blue
green with envy
rose-colored glasses
he was very green
turn red as a beet
tickled pink
heart of gold
he's yellow
turned purple
in the black
red tape

List 37: Animals

raining cats and dogs
monkey business
weasel out
go ape
let's talk turkey
let the cat out of the bag
crocodile tears
dark horse
card shark
whale of a time
drinks like a fish
frog in my throat
snake eyes
he's foxy
pig-headed
sounds fishy
make a hog of yourself
quit horsing around
he's a rat
he ratted on me
stool-pigeon
spring chicken

for the birds
eats like a bird
wolf in sheep's clothing
smell a rat
chicken-hearted
could eat a horse
don't monkey around
kill 2 birds with 1 stone
as the crow flies
cry wolf
dog-eared pages
let sleeping dogs lie
underdog
fish out of water
stir up a hornet's nest
get your goat
make a mountain out of a molehill
packed like sardines
black sheep
bird's eye view
wild-goose chase

List 38: Parts of Body

Head

can't make heads or tails of it
lost my head
keep your head above water
off the top of my head
head in the clouds
level-headed
head over heels
go through my head
have rocks in your head
put your heads together
use your head
hair is standing on end
up to his neck in work
tooth and nail
lump in my throat
save your neck
turn the other cheek
swallow your pride
my lips are sealed
slap in the face
blue in the face
face the music
keep a straight face
fall flat on your face
blow my mind
pick your brains
give you a piece of my mind

get on my nerves
boggle your mind
get up the nerve

Mouth

shoot off his mouth
down in the mouth
watch your mouth
foot in my mouth
big mouth
hand to mouth
keep a stiff upper lip
make my mouth water
word of mouth
leave a bad taste in your mouth
melt in your mouth
save your breath
take my breath away
catch your breath
skin of my teeth
sink my teeth into
on the tip of my tongue
eat your words
sharp tongue
mother tongue
slip of the tongue

Mouth (cont.)
tongue in cheek
tongue-tied

Eyes
only have eyes for you
never want to lay eyes on you
got my eye on you
make eyes
eyes popped
can't believe my eyes
more than meets the eye
sight for sore eyes
catch his eye
eyes are bigger than your stomach
feast your eyes on
pull the wool over his eyes
high brow

Nose
pay through the nose
turn up your nose
nose for news
by a nose (hair)
lead by the nose
keep your nose clean
nothing to sneeze at
under your nose

Ears
I'm all ears
ear-splitting
in one ear and out the other
keep an ear to the ground
prick up your ears

Hands
wind him around your little finger
finger in every pie
hands are tied
lend me a hand
give him a hand (applause)
green thumb
I'm all thumbs
at my fingertips
an old hand
have my hands full
wash my hands of
red-handed
slip through your fingers

upper hand
up in arms
hand-me-downs
hand it to you
hands off
thumb a ride
short-handed

Feet
toe the line
cold feet
he's a heel
shake a leg
pulling my leg
foot the bill
put your foot down
put your best foot forward
not a leg to stand on
drag one's feet
foot in the door
the shoe's on the other foot
step on one's toes

Trunk
chip on his shoulder
cold shoulder
get off my back
get it off your chest
elbow room
thorn in my side
turn your back on
turn my stomach
butterflies in my stomach
can't stomach it
lily-livered
make my flesh creep
busybody

Heart
heart to heart
learn by heart
have a heart
my heart's in my mouth
take to heart
hard-hearted
heart of stone
eat your heart out
break my heart
set your heart on

List 39: Other

ace in the hole
ahead of the game
all shook up
all washed up
asleep at the switch
as the crow flies
after a fashion
back seat driver
ball of fire
barking up the wrong tree
bark is worse than his bite
bats in your belfry
bawl out
beat around the bush
beat it
beauty sleep
bed of roses
behind the eight ball
beside himself
better late than never
big shot (cheese, wheel)
bite off more than you can chew
don't bite the hand that feeds you
bite the dust
blow your top (cool)
bone to pick
brush up on
build a fire under
burn the midnight oil
break your word
break the news
bury the hatchet
burns me up
by a hair
by hook or by crook
call it a day
call it quits
call the shots
can of worms
car pool
chicken out
chip off the old block
cook one's goose
crack up
crack a book
crack a joke
cramp your style
cream of the crop
cut corners
cut and dried
dead stop
dead to the world
die out
dime a dozen
do a double take

Don't bite off more than you can chew!

down in the dumps
dose of your own medicine
down the drain (tubes)
drag one's feet
draw a blank
draw the line
drive a hard bargain
drop in the bucket
eat like a bird (horse)
end of one's rope
feel like a million dollars
finders keepers
fit like a glove
flip one's lid
fly off the handle
fool around
fool proof
for keeps
fork out
forty winks
get away with
get down to brass tacks
get even
get off my back
get the ball rolling
get to the bottom of
get out of bed on the wrong side
ghost of a chance
give a hard time
give an inch and he'll take a mile
give yourself away
give up the ghost
globe trotter
go around in circles
go into orbit
go jump in the lake
go off the deep end
grass is always greener on the other side of the street

grin and bear it

ham it up

hang in there

hang ups

handwriting is on the wall

have a ball

have the last laugh

hold on to your hat (horses)

have your own way

have two strikes against you

high time

hit the nail on the head

hit the ceiling

hit below the belt

hit the sack (hay)

hold water

hold down a job

horse around

in the dark

in a nutshell

in one's hair

in the hole

in the same boat

in full swing

in hot water

in vain

irons in the fire

jack of all trades

jump down one's throat

just what the doctor ordered

keep the ball rolling

keep it under your hat

keep plugging away

kick in the pants

knock it off

kick the bucket

know the ropes

last straw

let off steam

lie down on the job

long shot

long winded

look daggers at

look down on

lose your shirt

lost cause

lower the boom

make fur fly

make a mountain out of a molehill

make ends meet

make yourself at home

man of his word

matter of life and death

monkey business

name is mud

needle in a haystack

old flame

once in a blue moon

on the house

on the lookout

on the bandwagon

on the ball

out of date

out of the question

out on a limb

paint the town red

pass the buck

pass out

penny for your thoughts

pick a fight

pins and needles

play second fiddle

pull yourself together

pinch pennies

play on words

pitch in

polish off

pop the question

polish the apple

pull strings

puppy love

put on your thinking cap

put your cards on the table

put the cart before the horse

put a feather in your cap

put all your eggs in one basket

rain cats and dogs

read between the lines

ring a bell

rob the cradle

rock the boat

red tape

rip off

rub the wrong way

rule of thumb

run down

security blanket

seeing is believing

separate men from the boys

shaking in his boots

sink or swim

sitting pretty

she slays me

stuffed shirt

ship shape

sleep on it

small talk

sound off

spaced out

spread like wildfire

spring chicken

stack the cards (deck)

start from scratch
steal his thunder
steal the spotlight
stick to your guns
stick-in-the-mud
strike it rich
strike home
strike while the iron is hot
take a back seat
take off
take your medicine
take the floor
take your hat off to
take sides
talk turkey
tall story
throw the book at
throw in the sponge (towel)
throw a.party
throw a fit
to the letter
time marches on
tie the knot
tickled to death
time of your life
touch and go
touch up
to the tune of

tricks of the trade
turn in
turn the tables
turn over a new leaf
turned on
twiddle your thumbs
under your wing
up to something
up in arms
ups and downs
upstage
wait on
walk all over
walk on air
walk on thin ice
warm the bench
wash dirty linen in public
waste your breath
wear and tear
wear out your welcome
when my ship comes in
weather the storm
writing on the wall
wind up
wipe out
word for word
word to the wise
zip your lip

List 40: Proverbs

Like father, like son.

OBJECTIVE

To develop the student's ability to understand the meanings of common proverbs used in language.

APPLICATIONS

- Discuss meanings of proverbs. Write proverbs on cards. Cut cards in half. Students match up parts of proverbs.

- Read some Aesop's fables. Have students make up a new fable to go with a proverb. They also may make up new proverbs.

- The students may act out Aesop's fables or improvise skits to illustrate other proverbs. These could be presented for other groups of classes.

1. Don't cry over spilt milk.
2. It never rains but it pours.
3. Don't count your chickens until they're hatched.
4. The proof of the pudding is in the eating.
5. He who laughs last, laughs best.
6. He who hesitates is lost.
7. Look before you leap.
8. A bird in the hand is worth two in the bush.
9. When the cat's away, the mice will play.
10. A rolling stone gathers no moss.
11. Strike while the iron is hot.
12. A penny saved is a penny earned.
13. Beggars should not be choosers.
14. Like father, like son.
15. You may lead a horse to water, but you can't make him drink.
16. All that glitters is not gold.
17. A stitch in time saves nine.
18. A fool and his money are soon parted.
19. A watched pot never boils.
20. Never look a gift horse in the mouth.
21. Birds of a feather flock together.
22. Too many cooks spoil the broth.

23. You cannot have your cake and eat it too.

24. A barking dog never bites.

25. Make hay while the sun shines.

26. Rome wasn't built in a day.

27. When in Rome, do as the Romans do.

28. Absence makes the heart grow fonder.

29. The early bird catches the worm.

30. A new broom sweeps clean.

31. The pot calls the kettle black.

32. People who live in glass houses shouldn't throw stones.

33. One good turn deserves another.

34. A friend in need is a friend indeed.

35. Two wrongs do not make a right.

36. The pen is mightier than the sword.

37. Curiosity killed the cat.

38. Necessity is the mother of invention.

39. Actions speak louder than words.

40. Haste makes waste.

41. Every cloud has a silver lining.

42. Beauty is only skin deep.

43. You can't teach an old dog new tricks.

44. Don't cross the bridge until you come to it.

45. All work and no play makes Jack a dull boy.

46. Money burns a hole in your pocket.

47. Don't change horses in the middle of the stream.

48. Every dog has his day.

49. Let sleeping dogs lie.

50. Little pitchers have big ears.

51. Many hands make light work.

52. Leave no stone unturned.

53. An apple a day keeps the doctor away.

54. Live and let live.

55. Don't kill the goose that lays the golden egg.

Lists 41–42: Scrambled Sentence Sequence

OBJECTIVE

To develop the student's ability to identify the correct logical order of sentences presented orally.

APPLICATIONS

• Read the sentences in the order given. Student decides if they are in the correct order. If not, he should repeat them in correct sequence. If he is incorrect, repeat the sentences again and give him a second try.

• Print the sentences on index card strips. Student must arrange them in order. Put a code on the back for self-checking.

• After ordering the sentences, the student tells what would happen next.

• Students may make up their own sequences to use with other students. Use pictures from your file as topic suggestions.

• Print sentences on index card strips and cut up into words and/or phrases. Student arranges words into sentences and then sentences in sequence. (Suggest that he find all words with capital letters and punctuation first.)

List 41: 2-Sentence Sequence

1. My coat got wet.
   It started to rain.

2. I told Tony a joke.
   Tony laughed.

3. The glass of milk spilled.
   Sue bumped the table.

4. Humpty Dumpty broke.
   Humpty Dumpty fell off the wall.

5. John jumped into the pool.
   There was a big splash.

6. The basketball went through the hoop.
   Danny threw the basketball.

7. Jack climbed up the beanstalk.
   Jack was very tired.

8. I patted the dog.
   The dog bit me.

9. Jay washed the dishes.
   Jay cleared the dishes off the table.

10. Cindy read the newspaper.
    Cindy threw the newspaper away.

11. The passengers stepped out of the airplane.
    The airplane landed.

12. Chris sat on the balloon.
    The balloon popped.

13. Juanita fell down.
    Juanita stepped on the banana peel.

14. The plant grew big.
    Jacob planted a plant.

15. Ellen lay down.
    Ellen fell asleep.

16. The bear chased the deer.
    The bear saw the deer.

17. I made some bread dough.
    I put the bread dough in the oven.

18. Snow began to fall.
    The streets filled with snow.

19. Snoopy felt full.
    Snoopy ate lots of dog food.

20. Joe jumped the highest.
    Joe received a blue ribbon.

21. Randy poured milk on the cereal.
    The cereal was dry.

22. Jimmy got on his bike.
    Jimmy had an accident.

23. The pig built a straw house.
    The wolf blew the house down.

24. José watched Sesame Street.
    José turned on the TV.

25. The wind blew hard.
    A tree fell down.

26. I got sunburned.
    I sat in the sun.

27. I ate the apple.
    I peeled the apple.

28. Lisa got on the school bus.
    Lisa waited for the bus.

29. We ate the cookies.
    We made chocolate chip cookies.

30. I got in the barber's chair.
    The barber cut my hair.

31. Cindy made a basket.
    The basketball game started.

32. Ali put on his boxing gloves.
    Ali won the boxing match.

33. The clown did funny tricks.
    The clown put on his costume.

34. Our dog chased a cat.
    The cat ran away.

35. The plane flew very high.
    The pilot got into his plane.

List 42: 3-Sentence Sequence

		Correct Order
1.	They went over a fence.	3
	The horse started to run.	2
	Maria got on her horse.	1
2.	Everyone cheered for him.	3
	The boys were playing baseball.	1
	Phil hit a home run.	2
3.	The sun melted the snow.	3
	There was a snowstorm.	1
	The ground was covered with snow.	2
4.	Bill gave me an orange.	1
	We ate it.	3
	I peeled it.	2
5.	A monkey did tricks.	2
	We went to the zoo.	1
	We laughed.	3
6.	Mom put candles on it.	2
	Amy blew out the candles.	3
	Mom baked a birthday cake.	1
7.	The firemen put out the fire.	3
	The fire broke out.	1
	We called the fire department.	2
8.	She mailed it.	3
	Judy wrote a letter.	1
	She put a stamp on it.	2
9.	The robber went into the bank.	1
	The police came.	3
	He stole some money.	2
10.	The rocket blasted off.	1
	It traveled through space.	2
	It landed on the moon.	3
11.	We said "trick or treat."	2
	We got some candy.	3
	We put on our costumes.	1
12.	Juan jumped in it.	3
	Juan saw a puddle.	2
	It rained very hard.	1
13.	Mother bird brought a worm.	3
	The egg cracked open.	1
	The bird got out.	2

Correct Order

14. The alarm clock rang. `1`
    I was late for school. `3`
    I went back to sleep. `2`

15. It flew over my house. `2`
    The airplane landed. `3`
    The airplane took off. `1`

16. Sam ate fifteen cookies. `1`
    Sam got a tummy ache. `2`
    Sam went to bed. `3`

17. He pulled my tooth. `3`
    I had a toothache. `1`
    I went to the dentist. `2`

18. He ate one. `2`
    Abe had three apples. `1`
    He had two left. `3`

19. Kim drank the milk. `3`
    The cow gave milk. `1`
    The farmer delivered the milk. `2`

20. Dan put on his parachute. `1`
    He jumped out of the airplane. `2`
    Dan landed safely. `3`

21. The team made a touchdown. `3`
    The football game started. `1`
    Joe kicked the ball hard. `2`

22. Betty threw a stick. `1`
    Snoopy brought it to Kim. `3`
    Snoopy ran after it. `2`

23. I put a slice of bread in the toaster. `2`
    I buttered the toast. `3`
    I opened the bread package. `1`

24. The candle burned. `2`
    Bill lit the candle. `1`
    The flame went out. `3`

25. Denise ate the apple. `3`
    The apple fell off the tree. `1`
    Denise picked it up. `2`

26. Chris cut out the material. `1`
    Chris wore the shirt he made. `3`
    Chris sewed on the sewing machine. `2`

27. A spider sat by Miss Muffet. `2`
    Miss Muffet ate her food. `1`
    Miss Muffet ran away. `3`

28. Goldilocks ran home. `3`
    Goldilocks ate the bears' porridge. `1`
    Goldilocks fell asleep. `2`

29. The prince married Cinderella. `3`
    Cinderella went to the ball. `1`
    Cinderella lost her slipper. `2`

		Correct Order
30.	The fox ate the Gingerbread Man.	3
	He jumped out of the oven.	2
	The old lady baked a Gingerbread Man.	1
31.	The caterpillar crawled onto the tree.	1
	A butterfly flew out.	3
	It made a cocoon.	2
32.	The boat was sailing on the lake.	1
	A storm blew up.	2
	The boat sank in the lake.	3
33.	Snoopy chased the robber.	3
	Snoopy was sleeping.	1
	Snoopy heard a robber.	2
34.	Paul bought a present.	1
	He gave it to Joe.	3
	He wrapped it.	2
35.	I bought spaghetti.	2
	I went to the store.	1
	I cooked dinner.	3
36.	John swam thirty laps.	3
	John dove into the pool.	2
	John put on his swimming suit.	1
37.	The fireman went to the fire.	3
	The fireman heard the alarm.	1
	He put on his hat and coat.	2
38.	Juanita caught a fish.	3
	She put the line in the water.	2
	Juanita put a worm on the fishhook.	1
39.	We ate dinner.	3
	We went to the restaurant.	1
	We ordered hamburgers.	2
40.	Bill and Betty got a new puppy.	1
	He went to sleep.	3
	They fed him some dog food.	2
41.	Ben went for a ride.	3
	He put a saddle on the horse.	2
	Ben got a new horse.	1
42.	Joan rolled the ball.	2
	Joan picked up the bowling ball.	1
	It knocked down all the pins.	3
43.	Stephanie chased her mouse.	3
	Stephanie opened the mouse cage.	1
	The mouse ran out.	2
44.	The farmer took the eggs to market.	3
	The hens laid eggs.	1
	The farmer took the eggs from the nests.	2
45.	Jimmy fell off his bike.	1
	Jimmy broke his leg.	2
	Jimmy went to the hospital.	3

Lists 43–46: Incomplete Sentences

OBJECTIVE

To develop the student's ability to supply appropriate words in sentences using context and/or phoneme clues.

Pinocchio grew a long _____.

APPLICATIONS

♦ Read the sentence and ask the student to say *any* appropriate word for the missing word. Encourage divergent responses.

♦ Put up an alphabet strip. Read the sentence and point to the first letter of the missing word. The student should give an appropriate word beginning with that letter.

　　Example: The boat is on the (*lake, lagoon*).

Instead of pointing to a letter, give the first phoneme as a clue. A clicker may be used to signify the missing word.

♦ Use stories children have written or dictated. Read them aloud and omit key words. The students supply appropriate words.

♦ Refer to List 2, Rhyming Sentences, for a similar missing word activity.

List 43: Level I

1. The boat is on the l_____.
2. The circus has funny c_____.
3. Can you ride a b_____?
4. A sport I like is b_____.
5. In summer we go on a v_____.
6. King Kong is a huge g_____.
7. Harry fell and broke his a_____.
8. Thunder makes a loud n_____.
9. Children should drink a lot of m_____.
10. Are you afraid of the d_____?
11. The beach is at the o_____.
12. I have saved a lot of m_____.
13. August is a hot m_____.
14. I ordered a pizza at the r_____.
15. The catcher caught the b_____.
16. The magician did a t_____.
17. We went to see a good m_____.
18. Last night we looked at the s_____.

19. Robert's car has a flat t_____.

20. The monkey was swinging through the t_____.

21. The cows are in the b_____.

22. Rosie knows how to cook t_____.

23. There are lots of stars in the s_____.

24. Put your dolls in the t_____.

25. We like to go s_____.

List 44: Level II

1. The werewolf has big f_____.
   He scares p_____.

2. Don't jump on the b_____.
   It might b_____.

3. The monkey is in the z_____.
   He likes to eat b_____.

4. I want a football for my b_____.
   My birthday is in S_____.

5. Pinocchio told many l_____.
   He grew a big n_____.

6. Bambi was a f_____.
   He played in the f_____.

7. The batter hit a h_____.
   Everyone stood up and ch_____.

8. I like to play b_____.
   I am on a t_____.

9. Snoopy has big e_____.
   He sleeps on his d_____.

10. Lions live in the j_____.
    They are very f_____.

11. Polar bears live where it is c_____.
    They swim in the o_____.

12. Jean planted a g_____.
    She grew tomatoes and b_____.

13. Where is your b_____?
    Bring it to m_____.

14. I love to eat s_____.
    It is my favorite f_____.

15. Popsicles taste good in the s_____.
    They are very c_____.

16. The eagle flew over the m_____.
    He landed on his n_____.

17. The hungry donkeys ate the h_____.
    Then they went to s_____.

18. My dog chews on b_____.
    He likes to eat d_____.

19. Willy Wonka had a huge chocolate f_____.
    He made lots of c_____.

20. Lizards run very f_____.
    They like to eat b_____.

21. Let's go fly our k_____.
    I bet mine will go very h_____.

22. Mickey Mouse has big e_____.
    We watch him on t_____.

23. Sam gave his dog a b_____.
    Then he gave him a b_____.

24. Jack won the running r_____.
    The judge gave him a p_____.

25. The secretary typed a l_____.
    She put it in an e_____.

List 45: Level III

1. Where does your little b_____ sleep?

2. My sister is s_____ with the measles.

3. What kind of c_____ do you like?

4. The caterpillar c_____ along the branch.

5. Do you have the k_____ to this door?

6. The horses were r_____ along the path.

7. I can't r_____ where I put my money.

8. Dan got a new s_____ bag for camping.

9. Jeff got a d_____ license.

10. My dad is s_____ feet tall.

11. Ima rode her h_____ to town.

12. Susie wrapped a p_____ for her grandmother.

13. Goldilocks t_____ the mother bear's porridge.

14. In the w_____ we go sledding down the hill.

15. Paul bought a furry m_____ for a pet.

16. I listen to m_____ on my stereo.

17. Don't b_____ this new glass.

18. My new coat c_____ twenty-five dollars.

19. Phil plays a t_____ in the school band.

20. The mother h_____ hatched five baby chicks.

21. John b_____ his leg while skiing.

22. The monster s_____ the little boy.

23. I heard a bird s_____ in the tree.

24. A surfer rides a w_____ into shore.

25. Would you l_____ butter on your toast?

List 46: Level IV

1. Bears s_____ all winter in caves.
   They wake up in the s_____.

2. Squirrels hide n_____ in hollow trees.
   They e_____ them in winter.

3. The tiger has s_____ on his back.
   He eats other a_____.

4. The fish saw the w_____ on the hook.
   He tried to b_____ it.

5. Cinderella lost her s_____ at midnight.
   The p_____ found it.

6. We saw a c_____ at the circus.
   He had a big red n_____.

7. The football player k_____ the ball.
   His team w_____ the game.

8. The deer ran from the f_____ fire.
   The fire b_____ down many trees.

9. The scouts set up their t_____ by the lake.
   They went s_____ the next day.

10. A kangaroo keeps her b_____ in her pouch.
    She can leap very h_____.

11. The shiny black seal dove under the w_____.
    He a_____ a fish.

12. The earthquake sh_____ the building.
    All the windows were b_____.

13. Have you ever w_____ a boxing match?
    The b_____ wears gloves and trunks.

14. The f_____ leaped out of the water.
    He caught a b_____ in his mouth.

15. Did you see the j_____ at the airport?
    It made a lot of n_____.

16. The s_____ fought in the war.
    Some of them got h_____.

17. The mother bird found a w_____ for her babies.
    It was l_____ and thin.

18. Delores b_____ a delicious cake.
    She decorated it with blue i_____.

19. The peanuts were e_____ by the elephants.
    The elephants picked them up with their t_____.

Incomplete Sentences (continued)

20. The Easter eggs were c_____ by the children.
    They were green, red and b_____.

21. Did you eat l_____ in the cafeteria?
    What did you e_____ today?

22. The coach blew his wh_____.
    The team s_____ playing.

23. Do you like to d_____ at night?
    I do t_____.

24. On the m_____ the astronauts picked up rocks.
    They brought them back to e_____.

25. What t_____ do you go to school?
    Do you eat b_____ first?

Lists 47–49: Following Directions

OBJECTIVE

To develop the student's ability to understand and follow oral directions and to give oral directions with precise language.

APPLICATIONS

+ Play "Simon Says" while giving the directions on the following lists. First select one child and give him the directions to follow.

+ Give the directions *first* and then select a child to perform them. This activity encourages all children to listen carefully.

+ After the directions are given and executed, have other children decide if the directions were followed correctly.

+ Let students make up their own directions to give to other students.

+ See List 49, Giving and Following Directions.

List 47: Following 2 Directions

Needed: 1 pencil, 1 book, chair, table, chalkboard

1. Snap your fingers.
   Clap your hands.

2. Stand up.
   Sit down.

3. Jump up.
   Hop on one foot.

4. Kneel down.
   Touch your head.

5. Raise your arms.
   Tap your nose.

6. Lift your feet.
   Stick out your tongue.

7. Close your eyes.
   Say your name.

8. Wink your eye.
   Wave your hand.

9. Pull your hair.
   Point your finger up.

10. Whistle.
    Touch your chin.

11. Point to the door.
    Touch your fingers together.

12. Touch the chair.
    Look at the ceiling.

13. Hum a tune.
    Shake your head.

14. Hold the pencil over your head.
    Raise your eyebrows.

15. Open your mouth.
    Wiggle your tongue.

16. Laugh.
    Put your hand over your mouth.

17. Jump two times.
    Slap your knee.

18. Touch your ear.
    Slap your elbow.

19. Lick your lips.
    Sniff.

20. Smile.
    Blink your eyes.

21. Point to your stomach.
    Cough.

22. Stand up on one foot.
    Touch your toes.

23. Put your hand on your shoulder.
    Cross your legs.

24. Tap the table with the pencil.
    Turn your head.

25. Slap your knees.
    Touch your nose.

26. Walk to the chalkboard.
    Put your hands on your head.

27. Put your hands over your eyes.
    Say your name.

28. Count to five.
    Point to the door.

29. Touch your heels.
    Whistle.

30. Open the book.
    Close your eyes.

31. Turn around 2 times.
    Pull your ear.

32. Click your teeth.
    Put your hands on your waist.

33. Walk around the table.
    Point to your toes.

34. Make a fist.
    Count to five.

35. Look at the floor.
    Touch your back.

List 48: Following 3 Directions

Starred (*) items may be done while seated.

Needed: pencil, book, cardboard tube, small bell, toy car, chalk, block, small box, beanbag, chair, table, chalkboard

* 1. Shake your wrist.
  Clap your hands.
  Ring the bell.

* 2. Stamp your feet.
  Look through the tube.
  Pat your stomach.

  3. Walk to the window.
  Put your hands on your head.
  Whistle.

  4. Take a deep breath.
  Turn around once.
  Touch your ankles.

  5. Make a fist.
  Cover your eyes.
  Walk backwards.

* 6. Put the pencil in the book.
  Roll the car.
  Pull your ear.

* 7. Roll the tube.
  Clap your hands.
  Make a wish.

  8. Jump two times.
  Say your last name.
  Pick up the car.

* 9. Wink your eye.
  Hum a tune.
  Click your fingers.

  10. Skip to the window.
  Hop twice.
  Sit on the floor.

  11. Go to the chalkboard.
  Draw a circle.
  Turn around once.

  12. Pick up the pencil.
  Put it on my desk.
  Knock on the door.

  13. Draw a circle in the air.
  Knock on the table.
  Make a 3 on the board with chalk.

*14. Hand me the car.
  Look through the tube.
  Give a block to ___(name)___.

  15. Throw the beanbag in the box.
  Ring the bell.
  Kneel down.

*16. Put the car on the book.
  Scratch your chin.
  Laugh.

  17. Walk around your chair.
  Put the bell beside the book.
  Touch your toes.

  18. Turn the box over.
  Put the bell on top of the box.
  Walk to the door.

  19. Put the pencil in the tube.
  Stand on one foot.
  Sit on the floor.

*20. Ring the bell.
  Put the block behind the box.
  Scratch your head.

*21. Put the car on the block.
  Touch your toes.
  Hum.

*22. Whistle.
  Slap your knee.
  Put the bell in the box.

*23. Say your name.
  Give the beanbag to me.
  Open the book.

  24. Put the tube under the table.
  Say your name.
  Sit by the chair.

  25. Hop on your left foot.
  Count to five.
  Ring the bell.

List 49: Giving and Following Directions

Equipment needed: 2 sets made up of the following:

1 large blue block
1 small blue block
1 flat red triangle
1 flat yellow triangle
1 toy car
2 plastic animals
(other items may be substituted)
1 table divider

1.

- Have two students sit side-by-side at the table. Put a divider between them on the table. Arrange a set of objects as pictured in illustration 1 in front of one student. He gives directions to the other student for setting up his objects in an identical arrangement.

- Start with three of the objects and increase the number as the students progress. Encourage use of specific spatial and identifying terms. Demonstrate first.

  Example: Put the large blue block on the left side of the table.

  Put the small blue block in front of the large blue block.

  Put the toy duck on the large blue block facing you.

  Etc.

2.

- Remove the divider and let the students check the work. Give them feedback on how to be more specific in giving directions and in following directions.

- Tape record the directions as given and replay them for checking performance.

Lists 50–51: Synonyms

Rabbit's seat—hare chair

OBJECTIVE

To develop the student's ability to understand and use appropriate synonyms in the language.

APPLICATIONS

♦ Demonstrate one set of rhyming synonyms.

♦ Read the phrase in part 1. Student should guess the rhyming synonym. If he has difficulty, ask for the easiest word.

> Example: HAPPY FATHER
>
> "What's another word for father?"
>
> "Dad."
>
> "Good. What's another word for happy? It sounds like *dad.*"
>
> "Glad. Glad dad."

♦ Introduce two or three new ones each day on the chalkboard for students to figure out.

♦ Let students take a list home and try them out on their families. They may make more up at home.

♦ Refer to List 1, Phonograms, to help students make new rhyming synonym pairs.

List 50: Rhyming Synonyms

Part 1	Part 2
angry boy	mad lad
happy father	glad dad
leftover glue	waste paste
sugary snack	sweet treat
ill hen	sick chick
police store	cop shop
warm bed	hot cot
noon-meal drink	lunch punch
enjoyable jog	fun run
wet hobo	damp tramp
summer-month song	June tune
fat newlywed	wide bride
grumpy man's sofa	grouch couch
pork jelly	ham jam
insect's trousers	ant's pants
rabbit's seat	hare chair
quick explosion	fast blast

Part 1 (cont.)

tardy boyfriend

dog kiss

three-wheeler journey

courageous servant

light-red beverage

cozy carpet

jet runway

submerged trash

tiny bouncer

night-bird scream

stranded vehicle

insect medicine

artificial rattler

identical label

extra cub

junk money

overweight rodent

smashed headcover

pottery platter

scary nightmare

stinker's bed

skinny relative

monarch's jewelry

hobo winner

tent light

great musical group

transparent ale

unexciting bone

galactic contest

choice hour

extensive tune

fast sweeper

upset thief

circular hill

uninteresting crustacean

high barrier

unhappy villain

sheep lift

docile fire

orderly chair

elf battle

Part 2 (cont.)

late date

pooch smooch

trike hike

brave slave

pink drink

snug rug

plane lane

sunk junk

small ball

owl howl

stuck truck

bug drug

fake snake

same name

spare bear

trash cash

fat rat

flat hat

clay tray

scream dream

skunk bunk

thin kin

king's rings

tramp champ

camp lamp

grand band

clear beer

dull skull

space race

prime time

long song

zoom broom

shook crook

round mound

drab crab

tall wall

sad cad

ram tram

tame flame

neat seat

sprite fight

List 51: Advanced Rhyming Synonyms

Part 1	Part 2
fortunate fowl	lucky ducky
humorous rabbit	funny bunny
untamed kid	wild child
huge patron	giant client
20-ton car	heavy Chevy
king's barbeque	royal broil
happy fruit	merry cherry
tiresome night noise	boring snoring
bloody tale	gory story
wedding vehicle	marriage carriage
funny cat	witty kitty
splendid treat	dandy candy
monster movie	creature feature
sticky stomach	gummy tummy
sea-water medicine	ocean potion
prison letter	jail mail
cow fight	cattle battle
silly flower	crazy daisy
iron teapot	metal kettle
wicked fight	cruel duel
cat's glove	kitten mitten
sick hen	stricken chicken
praying hockey player	holy goalie
devilish sailor	demon seaman
precipitation bucket	hail pail
delicate escargot	frail snail
sour southern dessert	bitter fritter
hill water display	mountain fountain

IV. Thinking with Language (cognitive)

52. Analogies, characteristics
53. Analogies, part–whole
54. Analogies, whole–part
55. Analogies, location
56. Analogies, action–object
57. Analogies, agent–action or object
58. Analogies, class or synonym
59. Analogies, familial
60. Analogies, grammatical
61. Analogies, temporal–sequential
62. Analogies, antonym
63. Categories, level I
64. Categories, level II
65. Classification, level I
66. Classification, level II

67. Classification, level III
68. Classification, level IV
69. Part-whole relationships, level I
70. Part-whole relationships, level II
71. Associations, level I
72. Associations, level II
73. Associations, level III
74. Similarities–differences, level I
75. Similarities–differences, level II
76. Absurd sentences, level I
77. Absurd sentences, level II
78. Inferences, level I
79. Inferences, level II
80. Logical sequences

Lists 52–62: Analogies

OBJECTIVE

To develop the student's ability to determine the logical relationships in analogies and supply the appropriate missing words.

APPLICATIONS

• Discuss the rule for analogies which is to determine the relationship in the first part and extend to the second part. Present one list at a time to teach similar relationships (whole–part, etc.).

• On a beginning level, use this presentation:

An *apple* is *red;* an *elephant* is _____.

Later introduce the more difficult presentation:

Apple is to *red* as *elephant* is to _____.

• On a more advanced level, give an incorrect analogy and let the student correct it telling why it is wrong.

An *apple* is *red;* an *elephant* is *big.* (not a color)

• Mix up analogies from different lists when students are successful at preceding activities. Write the analogies on cards for use at learning centers or for practicing with a visual cue.

• Have the students make up analogies at home as a family activity. Put these on cards to use at school. Write the student's name on the card as the contributor.

• Refer to List 63, Categories, and List 74, Similarities and Differences, to construct more analogies.

List 52: Characteristics

1. *Apple* is to *red* as *elephant* is to _____. grey

2. *Desk* is to *rectangle* as *bowl* is to _____. circle

3. *Towel* is to *fuzzy* as *paper* is to _____. smooth

4. *Day* is to *light* as *night* is to _____. dark

5. *Red* is to *stop* as *green* is to _____. go

6. *Pudding* is to *soft* as *cookie* is to _____. hard

7. *Tire* is to *rubber* as *bumper* is to _____. metal

8. *Window* is to *glass* as *dress* is to _____. cloth

9. *Ocean* is to *wet* as *desert* is to _____. dry

Analogies (continued)

10. *Point* is to *star* as *curve* is to _____.

11. *Coat* is to *fur* as *magazine* is to _____.

12. *Cow* is to *tame* as *fox* is to _____.

13. *Knife* is to *metal* as *shoe* is to _____.

14. *Sandpaper* is to *rough* as *glass* is to _____.

15. *Refrigerator* is to *cold* as *stove* is to _____.

16. *Tree* is to *green* as *snow* is to _____.

17. *Sun* is to *gas* as *moon* is to _____.

18. *Hero* is to *brave* as *coward* is to _____.

19. *Bread* is to *flour* as *wagon* is to _____.

20. *Carrot* is to *orange* as *strawberry* is to _____.

21. *Lemon* is to *sour* as *orange* is to _____.

22. *Lightning* is to *bright* as *thunder* is to _____.

23. *Scream* is to *loud* as *whisper* is to _____.

24. *Nail* is to *straight* as *hook* is to _____.

25. *Wool* is to *blanket* as *glass* is to _____.

circle

paper

wild

leather

smooth

hot

white

rock

scared

metal

red

sweet

loud

soft

bent

window

List 53: Part/Whole

1. *Shell* is to *egg* as *skin* is to _____.
2. *Cap* is to *bottle* as *lid* is to _____.
3. *Wing* is to *bird* as *arm* is to _____.
4. *Fingernail* is to *finger* as *buckle* is to _____.
5. *Keys* are to *piano* as *strings* are to _____.
6. *Second* is to *minute* as *minute* is to _____.
7. *Blood* is to *person* as *sap* is to _____.
8. *Hand* is to *arm* as *foot* is to _____.
9. *Pint* is to *quart* as *quart* is to _____.
10. *Petal* is to *flower* as *branch* is to _____.
11. *Hands* are to *clock* as *dial* is to _____.
12. *Apple* is to *tree* as *grape* is to _____.
13. *Column* is to *newspaper* as *paragraph* is to _____.
14. *Fin* is to *rocket* as *rudder* is to _____.
15. *Mate* is to *ship's crew* as *musician* is to _____.
16. *Skin* is to *man* as *hide* is to _____.
17. *Handle* is to *hammer* as *sole* is to _____.
18. *City* is to *state* as *state* is to _____.
19. *Backstop* is to *baseball diamond* as *goalpost* is to _____.
20. *Verse* is to *song* as *stanza* is to _____.
21. *Sailor* is to *Navy* as *soldier* is to _____.
22. *Cactus* is to *desert* as *vines* are to _____.
23. *Crust* is to *pie* as *icing* is to _____.
24. *Speck* is to *dust* as *sliver* is to _____.
25. *Pincers* are to *crab* as *claws* are to _____.

apple

can

person

belt

guitar

hour

tree

leg

gallon

tree

telephone

vine

book

boat

band

cow

shoe

country

football field

poem

Army

jungle

cake

wood

cat

Analogies (continued)

List 54: Whole/Part

1. *Forest* is to *log* as a *mine* is to _____.
2. *Dog* is to *mouth* as *bird* is to _____.
3. *Tiger* is to *stripes* as *leopard* is to _____.
4. *Deer* is to *antlers* as *elephant* is to _____.
5. *Person* is to *hands* as *dog* is to _____.
6. *Snail* is to *shell* as *camel* is to _____.
7. *Hand* is to *wrist* as *foot* is to _____.
8. *Book* is to *page* as *sandwich* is to _____.
9. *Lemon* is to *rind* as *apple* is to _____.
10. *Tape recorder* is to *tape* as *phonograph* is to _____.
11. *Ice skate* is to *blade* as *roller skate* is to _____.
12. *Eye* is to *pupil* as *cherry* is to _____.
13. *Head* is to *jaw* as *arm* is to _____.
14. *Orange* is to *peel* as *bread* is to _____.
15. *Snake* is to *fang* as *bee* is to _____.
16. *Guitar* is to *string* as *piano* is to _____.
17. *Horse* is to *hoof* as *seal* is to _____.
18. *Car* is to *steering wheel* as *bicycle* is to _____.
19. *Sentence* is to *words* as *paragraph* is to _____.
20. *Corn* is to *husk* as *banana* is to _____.
21. *Candle* is to *wick* as *firecracker* is to _____.
22. *Plant* is to *stem* as *tree* is to _____.
23. *Cat* is to *fur* as *porcupine* is to _____.
24. *Room* is to *floor* as *ship* is to _____.
25. *Turkey* is to *drumstick* as *pig* is to _____.

coal
beak
spots
tusks
paws
hump
ankle
meat
skin
record
wheel
pit
hand
crust
stinger
keys
flippers
handlebars
sentences
peel
fuse
trunk
quills
deck
pork chop

104

List 55: Location

1. *Boy* is to *bed* as *baby* is to _____.   crib

2. *Tablecloth* is to *table* as *rug* is to _____.   floor

3. *Meat* is to *butcher shop* as *cake* is to _____.   bakery

4. *Fish* is to *river* as *whale* is to _____.   ocean

5. *Teacher* is to *classroom* as *sailor* is to _____.   ship

6. *Judge* is to *courtroom* as *waiter* is to _____.   restaurant

7. *Bear* is to *den* as *owl* is to _____.   tree

8. *Water* is to *glass* as *coffee* is to _____.   cup

9. *Person* is to *house* as *bird* is to _____.   nest

10. *Fish* is to *river* as *coal* is to _____.   mine

11. *Hawaiian* is to *Hawaii* as *Texan* is to _____.   Texas

12. *Gun* is to *holster* as *dollar* is to _____.   wallet

13. *Grass* is to *ground* as *bark* is to _____.   tree

14. *People* are to *hotel* as *dogs* are to _____.   kennel

15. *Typewriter* is to *office* as *barbell* is to _____.   gym

16. *Fruit* is to *bowl* as *flowers* are to _____.   vase

17. *Chimney* is to *house* as *steeple* is to _____.   church

18. *Cactus* is to *desert* as *vines* are to _____.   jungle

19. *Eyebrows* are to *eyes* as *mustache* is to _____.   mouth

20. *Skier* is to *slopes* as *lumberjack* is to _____.   forest

21. *Photographer* is to *studio* as *teacher* is to _____.   classroom

22. *Boxer* is to *ring* as *scuba diver* is to _____.   ocean

23. *Plant* is to *nursery* as *shovel* is to _____.   hardware store

24. *Cowboy* is to *rodeo* as *clown* is to _____.   circus

25. *Ring* is to *finger* as *bracelet* is to _____.   wrist

List 56: Action/Object

1. *Drive* is to *car* as *fly* is to _____.   airplane
2. *Shoot* is to *gun* as *cut* is to _____.   knife
3. *Beat* is to *drum* as *blow* is to _____.   horn
4. *Lick* is to *ice cream cone* as *chew* is to _____.   steak
5. *Brush* is to *hair* as *wash* is to _____.   face
6. *Skate* is to *ice* as *ski* is to _____.   snow
7. *Zip* is to *jacket* as *lock* is to _____.   door
8. *Slide* is to *sled* as *roll* is to _____.   wagon
9. *Ring* is to *bell* as *honk* is to _____.   horn
10. *Digest* is to *stomach* as *breathe* is to _____.   lungs
11. *Sweep* is to *broom* as *scrub* is to _____.   mop
12. *Jump* is to *trampoline* as *somersault* is to _____.   mat
13. *Bake* is to *oven* as *boil* is to _____.   stove
14. *Paint* is to *brush* as *draw* is to _____.   pencil
15. *Touch* is to *finger* as *smell* is to _____.   nose
16. *Turn* is to *wheel* as *slide* is to _____.   drawer
17. *Sing* is to *mouth* as *walk* is to _____.   feet
18. *Swallow* is to *throat* as *blink* is to _____.   eye
19. *Drink* is to *milk* as *eat* is to _____.   bread
20. *Walk* is to *crutches* as *see* is to _____.   glasses
21. *Pick* is to *banjo* as *strum* is to _____.   guitar
22. *Listen* is to *stethoscope* as *look* is to _____.   microscope
23. *Kick* is to *football* as *bounce* is to _____.   basketball
24. *Sniff* is to *nose* as *wink* is to _____.   eye
25. *Read* is to *book* as *measure* is to _____.   ruler

List 57: Agent — Action or Object

1. *Lion* is to *roar* as *donkey* is to _____.   hee–haw

2. *Worm* is to *crawl* as *grasshopper* is to _____.   hop

3. *Man* is to *talk* as *duck* is to _____.   quack

4. *Bird* is to *fly* as *rabbit* is to _____.   hop

5. *Horse* is to *neigh* as *cow* is to _____.   moo

6. *Lizard* is to *crawl* as *swan* is to _____.   swim

7. *Pilot* is to *fly* as *jockey* is to _____.   ride

8. *Bee* is to *buzz* as *bird* is to _____.   chirp

9. *Feet* are to *walk* as *eyes* are to _____.   see

10. *Frog* is to *leap* as *horse* is to _____.   gallop

11. *Snake* is to *bite* as *wasp* is to _____.   sting

12. *Minister* is to *preach* as *golfer* is to _____.   play

13. *Barber* is to *trim* as *miner* is to _____.   dig

14. *Musician* is to *perform* as *zookeeper* is to _____. feed

15. *Optometrist* is to *refract* as *dentist* is to _____. drill

16. *Actor* is to *stage* as *nurse* is to _____.   hospital

17. *Judge* is to *law* as *referee* is to _____.   football

18. *Man* is to *footprints* as *deer* is to _____.   tracks

19. *Baker* is to *cake* as *secretary* is to _____.   letter

20. *Baby* is to *diapers* as *boy* is to _____.   pants

21. *Engineer* is to *train* as *milkman* is to _____.   truck

22. *Horse* is to *hay* as *tiger* is to _____.   meat

23. *Dog* is to *collar* as *woman* is to _____.   necklace

24. *King* is to *England* as *President* is to _____.   U.S.

25. *Architect* is to *house* as *author* is to _____.   book

26. *Sculptor* is to *statue* as *composer* is to _____. music

27. *Dog* is to *dog food* as *mouse* is to _____.   cheese

28. *Eye* is to *book* as *ear* is to _____.   record

29. *Physician* is to *man* as *veterinarian* is to _____. animal

30. *Firefighter* is to *hose* as *carpenter* is to _____. saw

List 58: Class or Synonym

1. *Laugh* is to *giggle* as *sob* is to _____.
2. *Shut* is to *slam* as *twist* is to _____.
3. *Massive* is to *large* as *observe* is to _____.
4. *Looked* is to *saw* as *screamed* is to _____.
5. *Cheap* is to *inexpensive* as *happy* is to _____.
6. *Courage* is to *bravery* as *bashfulness* is to _____.
7. *Present* is to *gift* as *ask* is to _____.
8. *Car* is to *vehicle* as *chair* is to _____.
9. *Robin* is to *bird* as *toaster* is to _____.
10. *Bear* is to *animal* as *brown* is to _____.
11. *Pear* is to *fruit* as *spinach* is to _____.
12. *Butterfly* is to *insect* as *donkey* is to _____.
13. *Sleep* is to *rest* as *jog* is to _____.
14. *Bear* is to *mammal* as *crocodile* is to _____.
15. *Turkey* is to *bird* as *bee* is to _____.
16. *Rocker* is to *chair* as *cradle* is to _____.
17. *Cup* is to *container* as *iron* is to _____.
18. *Recall* is to *remember* as *error* is to _____.
19. *Church* is to *building* as *diamond* is to _____.
20. *Golf* is to *sport* as *hammer* is to _____.
21. *Cake* is to *dessert* as *doll* is to _____.
22. *Christmas* is to *holiday* as *jacket* is to _____.
23. *Buy* is to *purchase* as *beautiful* is to _____.
24. *Ancient* is to *old* as *modern* is to _____.
25. *Chevrolet* is to *car* as *bakery* is to _____.

cry

turn

watch

yelled

merry

shyness

request

furniture

appliance

color

vegetable

animal

exercise

amphibian

insect

crib

metal

mistake

jewel

tool

toy

clothing

pretty

new

store

List 59: Familial

1. *Boy* is to *father* as *girl* is to _____.   mother
2. *Uncle* is to *male* as *aunt* is to _____.   female ·
3. *Horse* is to *colt* as *sheep* is to _____.   lamb
4. *Waiter* is to *waitress* as *nephew* is to _____.   niece
5. *Puppy* is to *dog* as *kitten* is to _____.   cat
6. *Uncle* is to *he* as *aunt* is to _____.   she
7. *King* is to *queen* as *prince* is to _____.   princess
8. *Tadpole* is to *frog* as *fawn* is to _____.   deer
9. *Kid* is to *goat* as *cub* is to _____.   bear
10. *Seedling* is to *plant* as *sapling* is to _____.   tree
11. *Caterpiller* is to *butterfly* as *calf* is to _____.   cow
12. *He* is to *she* as *him* is to _____.   her
13. *Duck* is to *duckling* as *hen* is to _____.   chick
14. *Rooster* is to *hen* as *husband* is to _____.   wife
15. *Aunt* is to *niece* as *uncle* is to _____.   nephew
16. *Chicken* is to *egg* as *mother* is to _____.   baby
17. *Bull* is to *cow* as *buck* is to _____.   doe
18. *Gosling* is to *goose* as *foal* is to _____.   horse
19. *Tigress* is to *tiger* as *nanny-goat* is to _____.   billy-goat
20. *Kid* is to *cub* as *goat* is to _____.   bear

List 60: Grammatical

1. *Fat* is to *fatter* as *big* is to _____.   bigger
2. *Look* is to *looked* as *shout* is to _____.   shouted
3. *Drink* is to *drank* as *swim* is to _____.   swam
4. *Sweep* is to *swept* as *find* is to _____.   found
5. *Do* is to *did* as *go* is to _____.   went
6. *Jump* is to *jumped* as *play* is to _____.   played
7. *Bite* is to *bit* as *chew* is to _____.   chewed
8. *Blow* is to *blew* as *feed* is to _____.   fed
9. *We* is to *our* as *you* is to _____.   your
10. *Man* is to *his* as *woman* is to _____.   hers/her
11. *When* is to *time* as *where* is to _____.   place
12. *Gave* is to *give* as *ran* is to _____.   run
13. *Met* is to *meet* as *shone* is to _____.   shine
14. *Him* is to *her* as *himself* is to _____.   herself
15. *Good* is to *better* as *bad* is to _____.   worse
16. *Mouse* is to *mice* as *goose* is to _____.   geese
17. *Knife* is to *knives* as *leaf* is to _____.   leaves
18. *I* is to *we* as *me* is to _____.   us
19. *Is not* is to *isn't* as *are not* is to _____.   aren't
20. *Man* is to *men* as *woman* is to _____.   women
21. *He* is to *him* as *she* is to _____.   her
22. *Boy* is to *boys* as *child* is to _____.   children
23. *Wife* is to *wives* as *sheep* is to _____.   sheep
24. *Shouldn't* is to *should not* as *wouldn't* is to _____.   would not
25. *Cannot* is to *can't* as *will not* is to _____.   won't
26. *Sleep* is to *slept* as *stick* is to _____.   stuck
27. *Feet* is to *foot* as *wolves* is to _____.   wolf
28. *Forgave* is to *forgive* as *chose* is to _____.   choose
29. *Meant* is to *mean* as *spread* is to _____.   spread
30. *I* is to *I'm* as *he* is to _____.   he's

List 61: Temporal Or Sequential

1. *April* is to *May* as *June* is to _____.   July
2. *Start* is to *finish* as *appetizer* is to _____.   dessert
3. *Afternoon* is to *night* as *fall* is to _____.   winter
4. *Head* is to *tail* as *engine* is to _____.   caboose
5. *Caterpiller* is to *butterfly* as *tadpole* is to _____.   frog
6. *Monday* is to *Wednesday* as *January* is to _____.   March
7. *F* is to *H* as *X* is to _____.   Z
8. *Fight* is to *win* as *search* is to _____.   find
9. *Lamb* is to *sheep* as *colt* is to _____.   horse
10. *Grape* is to *raisin* as *plum* is to _____.   prune
11. *Pig* is to *bacon* as *cow* is to _____.   steak
12. *Milk* is to *butter* as *wheat* is to _____.   bread
13. *2* is to *4* as *6* is to _____.   8
14. *Second* is to *minute* as *minute* is to _____.   hour
15. *5* is to *10* as *50* is to _____.   100
16. *February* is to *January* as *Saturday* is to _____.   Friday
17. *H* is to *G* as *P* is to _____.   O
18. *Thirsty* is to *drink* as *hungry* is to _____.   eat
19. *Nectar* is to *honey* as *pollen* is to _____.   wax
20. *Build* is to *cabin* as *dig* is to _____.   well
21. *Faint* is to *fall* as *cut* is to _____.   bleed
22. *Lightning* is to *thunder* as *fire* is to _____.   smoke
23. *15* is to *13* as *6* is to _____.   4
24. *First* is to *second* as *fourth* is to _____.   fifth
25. *Puppy* is to *dog* as *cub* is to _____.   bear

Analogies (continued)

List 62: Antonyms

1. *Pig* is to *dirty* as *cat* is to _____.   clean
2. *Man* is to *king* as *woman* is to _____.   queen
3. *Brick* is to *heavy* as *nail* is to _____.   light
4. *Sun* is to *morning* as *moon* is to _____.   night
5. *Turtle* is to *slow* as *rabbit* is to _____.   fast
6. *Bridge* is to *over* as *tunnel* is to _____.   under
7. *Two* is to *double* as *one* is to _____.   single
8. *Out* is to *exit* as *in* is to _____.   entrance
9. *Start* is to *begin* as *quit* is to _____.   end
10. *Jail* is to *guilty* as *freedom* is to _____.   innocent
11. *Increase* is to *add* as *decrease* is to _____.   subtract
12. *Good* is to *reward* as *bad* is to _____.   punish
13. *Sink* is to *rock* as *float* is to _____.   cork
14. *Summer* is to *warm* as *winter* is to _____.   cool
15. *Sugar* is to *sweet* as *pickle* is to _____.   sour
16. *Quiet* is to *whisper* as *loud* is to _____.   yell
17. *Right* is to *true* as *wrong* is to _____.   false
18. *Engine* is to *first* as *caboose* is to _____.   last
19. *Mouse* is to *small* as *elephant* is to _____.   large
20. *Above* is to *sky* as *below* is to _____.   ground
21. *Night* is to *sleep* as *morning* is to _____.   wake
22. *Minute* is to *short* as *hour* is to _____.   long
23. *Canada* is to *near* as *China* is to _____.   far
24. *Pull* is to *wagon* as *push* is to _____.   stroller
25. *Giggle* is to *laugh* as *sob* is to _____.   cry
26. *Top* is to *high* as *bottom* is to _____.   low
27. *Princess* is to *pretty* as *witch* is to _____.   ugly
28. *Girl* is to *she* as *boy* is to _____.   he
29. *Absent* is to *gone* as *present* is to _____.   here
30. *Hero* is to *brave* as *coward* is to _____.   scared

Lists 63–64: Categories

OBJECTIVE

To develop the student's ability to determine which words can be grouped into a category and why other words do not belong.

APPLICATIONS

◆ Say the words in Part 1. Student names the category to which they belong. He may also add another word in that category.

◆ Say two or more words from Part 1 and the word in Part 2. Student tells which does not belong and why.

◆ Use real objects or toys instead of words for a similar activity.

◆ Encourage divergent responses. There may be several possible answers to each set.

　　Example: BOOT, SANDAL, SHOE, SLIPPER

　　　　1. Slipper doesn't belong because it is worn primarily inside the house.

　　　　2. Sandal doesn't belong because it has straps.

　　　　3. Boot doesn't belong because it goes up high on the leg.

◆ Have children make up their own category sets.

◆ Refer to Lists 82 to 86, Body Language, to make up new category groups.

List 63: Level I

Part 1	Part 2
1. tugboat, raft, canoe	helicopter
2. church, store, school	stadium
3. fly, swim, run	sit
4. butterfly, moth bee	spider
5. wink, stare, blink	sneeze
6. freezing, cold, chilly	warm
7. frightened, scared, afraid	brave
8. happy, merry, joyful	angry
9. cup, dish, plate	fork
10. book, newspaper, magazine	pencil
11. lettuce, cabbage, peas	steak
12. James, John, Jim	Jane
13. red, black, purple	light
14. shoes, socks, skates	hat
15. tennis, golf, basketball	playground
16. violin, banjo, flute	radio

Categories (continued)

<table>
<tr><td colspan="2">Part 1 (cont.)</td><td>Part 2 (cont.)</td></tr>
<tr><td>17:</td><td>Sunday, Monday, Friday</td><td>January</td></tr>
<tr><td>18.</td><td>Halloween, 4th of July, Easter</td><td>presents</td></tr>
<tr><td>19.</td><td>bed, stove, lamp</td><td>kitchen</td></tr>
<tr><td>20.</td><td>man, girl, mother</td><td>bike</td></tr>
<tr><td>21.</td><td>toes, fingers, head</td><td>shoes</td></tr>
<tr><td>22.</td><td>car, bus, boat</td><td>table</td></tr>
<tr><td>23.</td><td>orange, peach, plum</td><td>potato</td></tr>
<tr><td>24.</td><td>meow, bark, moo</td><td>cat</td></tr>
<tr><td>25.</td><td>doctor, principal, baker</td><td>child</td></tr>
<tr><td>26.</td><td>cake, cookie, pie</td><td>milk</td></tr>
<tr><td>27.</td><td>radio TV, movie</td><td>book</td></tr>
<tr><td>28.</td><td>leaf, root, stem</td><td>garden</td></tr>
<tr><td>29.</td><td>arm, leg, shoulder</td><td>chair</td></tr>
<tr><td>30.</td><td>cloud, star, moon</td><td>building</td></tr>
<tr><td>31.</td><td>stove, refrigerator, sink</td><td>bed</td></tr>
<tr><td>32.</td><td>match, flashlight, sun</td><td>night</td></tr>
<tr><td>33.</td><td>ant, spider, cockroach</td><td>puppy</td></tr>
<tr><td>34.</td><td>scream, yell, talk</td><td>run</td></tr>
<tr><td>35.</td><td>desk, telephone, typewriter</td><td>secretary</td></tr>
<tr><td>36.</td><td>cough, sneeze, talk</td><td>run</td></tr>
<tr><td>37.</td><td>skis, snowshoes, sled</td><td>bicycle</td></tr>
<tr><td>38.</td><td>coat, sweater, jacket</td><td>pants</td></tr>
<tr><td>39.</td><td>ducks, chickens, geese</td><td>dog</td></tr>
<tr><td>40.</td><td>suitcase, trunk, purse</td><td>money</td></tr>
<tr><td>41.</td><td>dollar, penny, nickel</td><td>spend</td></tr>
<tr><td>42.</td><td>coke, juice, milk</td><td>cake</td></tr>
<tr><td>43.</td><td>horse, bicycle, tricycle</td><td>couch</td></tr>
<tr><td>44.</td><td>bottle, cup, glass</td><td>water</td></tr>
<tr><td>45.</td><td>box, sack, barrel</td><td>plate</td></tr>
<tr><td>46.</td><td>pin, knife, needle</td><td>yarn</td></tr>
<tr><td>47.</td><td>week, hour, second</td><td>clock</td></tr>
<tr><td>48.</td><td>rib, skull, collarbone</td><td>tongue</td></tr>
<tr><td>49.</td><td>fall, spring, summer</td><td>play</td></tr>
<tr><td>50.</td><td>shovel, hoe, rake</td><td>grass</td></tr>
</table>

List 64: Level II

	Part 1	Part 2	Difference
1.	pie, cookies, cake	ice cream	(cold dessert)
2.	boot, sandal, shoe	slipper	(wear inside)
3.	elephant, zebra, bear	horse	(farm animal)
4.	refrigerator, dishwasher, stove	sink	(not electric)
5.	television, movie, filmstrip	record	(no picture)
6.	crib, cradle, baby bed	hammock	(not for babies)
7.	bakery, department store, hardware store	theatre	(does not sell goods)
8.	baseball, golf, tennis	boxing	(no ball)
9.	lemonade, orange juice, limeade	milk	(not a juice)
10.	sun, moon, stars	cloud	(made of water)
11.	bench, stool, swing	cushion	(soft)
12.	slide, swing, jump rope	checkers	(use indoors)
13.	necklace, bracelet, ring	belt	(not jewelry)
14.	ice cream, jello, pudding	cookies	(not cold)
15.	cow, pig, horse	tiger	(jungle animal)
16.	bell, alarm, telephone	lamp	(no noise)
17.	camper, van, station wagon	convertible	(can fold top down)
18.	daisy, rose, petunia	ivy	(no flowers)
19.	arm, hand, fingers	chest	(on trunk)
20.	trailer, apartment, house	tent	(cloth)
21.	broom, mop, vacuum	dust pan	(no long handle)
22.	mosquito, bee, wasp	fly	(no sting)
23.	trumpet, trombone, saxophone	whistle	(not musical)
24.	referee, umpire, judge	coach	(does not judge)
25.	lion, tiger, leopard	bear	(not a cat)
26.	nickel, dime, quarter	penny	(not silver)
27.	windmill, ferris wheel, pencil sharpener	typewriter	(does not turn)
28.	glider, hot air balloon, hang glider	helicopter	(has a motor)
29.	sleigh, sled, toboggan	skis	(worn on feet)
30.	angry, annoyed, mad	amused	(happy feeling)
31.	opera, concert, symphony	stereo	(not a performance)
32.	water skiing, scuba diving, surfing	ice skating	(on frozen water)
33.	painter, drafter, cartoonist	sculptor	(does not usually use paper)
34.	actor, auctioneer, disk jockey	biographer	(writes)
35.	Japan, Australia, Russia	New York	(city)
36.	ounce, pound, ton	mile	(distance)

Categories (continued)

Part 1 (cont.)	Part 2 (cont.)	Difference (cont.)
37. Army, Navy, Marines	Boy Scouts	(for youth)
38. kick, hop, jump	pinch	(with fingers)
39. cub, kid, duckling	hen	(adult animal)
40. petal, stem, root	trunk	(part of tree)
41. jacket, sweater, coat	shirt	(worn under others)
42. moo, meow, bark	talk	(not animal noise)
43. fairy tale, mystery, poem	song	(musical)
44. pedals, kickstand, handlebars	steering wheel	(part of car)
45. pork chop, hamburger, roast	fishsticks	(not meat)
46. uncle, brother, grandfather	aunt	(woman)
47. strawberries, cherries, tomatoes	carrots	(not red)
48. milk, paste, glue	coke	(not white)
49. shout, talk, whisper	cough	(not form of talking)
50. rain, sleet, hail	tornado	(not precipitation)

Lists 65–68: Classification

OBJECTIVE

To develop the student's ability to name items that can be classified under one label.

APPLICATIONS

♦ Name a category label from the list. Have students brainstorm all items that could be classified under that label (see examples on p. 121). Encourage divergent responses. Give clues to elicit some items.

   Example: "Something you wear in the rain." (raincoat)

   List the items on a chart. Let students add to it when they think of new ones.

♦ Write a category label on a card with items written on the reverse side. Items can be read off and students guess the category, or name the category and guess items.

♦ Place 15 or 20 small objects or toys in a box. Have the students classify them into several suggested categories (wood, plastic, rubber); (red, wood, long). Students may also select their own category labels to classify under.

♦ Have students think up new Level IV categories for the class (2 characteristics).

♦ Send a category label home and ask families to work together classifying items under that label.

♦ Refer to Lists 82 through 87 for extended classifications.

List 65: Level I

Note: See examples on page 121.

1. clothes
2. colors
3. animals
4. drinks
5. cereals
6. TV programs
7. cartoon characters
8. boys' names
9. kinds of stores
10. kinds of jobs
11. tools
12. sports
13. kinds of dogs
14. fruits
15. furniture
16. holidays
17. kinds of insects
18. things in the kitchen
19. kinds of transportation

20. cold things
21. musical instruments
22. things on the playground
23. desserts
24. parts of the body
25. parts of a house
26. pets
27. storybook characters
28. vegetables
29. things you study at school
30. things you wear on your feet
31. things you wear on your head
32. hard things
33. soft things
34. places to keep money
35. things on your face
36. things you sit on
37. things that light up
38. things that make you laugh
39. parts of a bicycle
40. things that are hot
41. things that have a switch
42. kinds of animal noises
43. indoor games
44. things you shouldn't touch
45. things made of wood
46. things that are round
47. things made of paper
48. things used for cleaning
49. things that sting or bite
50. things in a circus

List 66: Level II

1. things associated with Halloween
2. kinds of flowers
3. parts of a pizza
4. types of books
5. things you can sleep on
6. liquids
7. kinds of trucks
8. building materials
9. baby animal names
10. things you wear when it's cold
11. things under the water
12. things in a jungle
13. States
14. kinds of meat
15. things made of water
16. kinds of fish
17. metals
18. things with heels
19. things you do with your legs
20. things you do with your hands
21. things that bounce
22. things you can sail on
23. kinds of precipitation or weather
24. kinds of buildings
25. things that hold other things
26. people who wear hats when they work
27. things that float
28. things you hunt
29. things that need a battery
30. creatures with shells
31. things you look through
32. animals with horns or tusks
33. quiet places
34. things underground
35. things with a blade
36. things that measure
37. things a magician uses
38. things found in a gym
39. things used by a secretary
40. things that people step on
41. things that are inflated
42. things that are circular
43. things that tell time
44. things that turn
45. things that rhyme with "hat"
46. things that are tiny
47. things in a parade
48. people in the "Wizard of Oz"
49. things that bend
50. things you pull

List 67: Level III

1. types of writings
2. names of planets
3. countries
4. cities
5. things that stick up out of water
6. things that have wrinkles
7. things that come in pairs
8. things you put together
9. things you pluck
10. things that absorb
11. things that get smaller when you use them
12. things with double letters
13. people in a courtroom
14. lonely places
15. things used in winter sports
16. kinds of music
17. parts of a castle
18. things that hold up other things
19. things that are not real
20. things you see in the spring
21. things that are brittle
22. Presidents of the U.S.
23. things you spray
24. things in a rodeo
25. things that you see at Christmas time
26. things that are clipped
27. measurements (oz., lb.)
28. directions (east, right)
29. things you roll up
30. ways animals move
31. groups to belong to
32. names of groups of animals
33. things used in wars
34. things that are painted
35. fishing equipment
36. things with lids
37. things you write with
38. things you do with your eyes (peer, wink)
39. things that have humps
40. things that are used in building construction
41. size words (huge, tiny, etc.)
42. kinds of speaking (yell, murmur, etc.)
43. things you put on walls
44. things used for cleaning
45. things that are very thin
46. things that are square
47. kinds of homes (apartment, burrow)
48. things that are silver
49. things that go up
50. people who work outdoors

List 68: Level IV (2 characteristics)

1. things that are long and thin (yardstick, asparagus, arrow, pencil, snake, etc.)
2. things that are round and hard (marble, gumballs, cannon ball, etc.)
3. things you sit on that are hard (bench, swing, floor, bleachers, etc.)
4. things you blow that are not musical instruments
5. vehicles that do not have motors
6. things that are soft and sticky
7. things that are round and used in games
8. things that are circular and turn
9. things that are plastic and used in the kitchen
10. things that are small and expensive
11. things that are red and eaten
12. things that are hard and slippery
13. foods that grow underground
14. things that break when you bend them
15. things that you cook but don't eat (bones, corn cobs, etc.)
16. things that are dry that you pour
17. things that are small and heavy
18. things that are white and flat
19. things that are liquid and white
20. foods that make noise when you chew

EXAMPLES

Level I — Clothes

hat	snowsuit
coat	jacket
scarf	skirt
blouse	shorts
socks	shoes
belt	poncho
pantyhose	raincoat
mittens	rainboots
sweater	cowboy boots
thongs	gloves
helmet	muffler
diapers	undershirt
cape	sandals

Level II — Things you do with your hands

grab	pinch
pick	clench
box	thump
stretch	hit
play	strum
close	wiggle
clasp	hold
lift	point
type	write
tap	shake
poke	clap
snap	pet
wash	rub

Level III — Types of writings

novel	poem
limerick	biography
mystery	fairy tale
haiku	science fiction
folk tale	fable
list	description
alphabet	tall tale
paragraph	research report
nonsense	scientific report
sentence	story
column	article
joke	riddle

Lists 69–70: Part-Whole Relationships

OBJECTIVE

To develop the student's ability to identify relationships between parts and wholes and learn related vocabulary and function concepts.

APPLICATIONS

• Name two or more parts of an object on Level 1 list. Student names the whole.

• Name the one part listed. Student names the whole and all other parts he can think of.

• Show a picture of the whole if available. Have the student name all the parts. Ask, "What is this?", "Where is the _____?", "What is it made of?", and "What is it used for?". Let one student be the teacher and ask the others questions.

• Encourage divergent responses. If possible, use real objects for the student to examine carefully.

Example: Have the student look at his own *hand* and name parts:

skin	fingernails	bones
knuckles	blood	muscles
veins	thumb	scar
lifeline	fingers	wrinkles
"half-moon"	hangnail	cuticle

This is a good way to expand vocabulary.

• Make lists of wholes and parts to match. Laminate for repeated use.

List 69: Level I

Part — Whole
1. dial — telephone
2. propeller — airplane
3. steering wheel — car
4. collar — shirt
5. feathers — bird
6. pedals — bicycle
7. shower — bathroom
8. paw — dog
9. candles — birthday cake
10. hand — arm
11. branch — tree
12. shelf — bookcase
13. keys — piano
14. pages — book
15. words — sentence
16. letters — word
17. sail — sailboat
18. chimney — house
19. son — family

Part — Whole
20. fingers — hand
21. floor — room
22. stove — kitchen
23. switch — lamp
24. tongue — mouth
25. closet — bedroom
26. crosswalk — street
27. frosting — cake
28. crust — pie
29. shell — egg
30. horns — bull
31. roots — plant
32. beak — bird
33. blade — knife
34. morning — day
35. sand — beach
36. beds — hospital
37. drawers — desk
38. backstop — baseball diamond

39. peel — banana
40. stinger — bee
41. trees — jungle (forest)
42. twigs — nest
43. chain — swing
44. engine — car
45. pants — suit
46. screen — TV set
47. months — year
48. minutes — hour
49. battery — flashlight
50. spokes — wheel
51. roof — house
52. mattress — bed
53. hoofs — horse
54. stem — flower
55. soldier — Army
56. cap — bottle
57. microphone — tape recorder

58. cash register — store
59. light bulb — lamp
60. Arizona (or your state) — United States
61. stomach — body
62. nose — face
63. pinecone — tree
64. button — shirt
65. siren — police car (fire engine)
66. bread — sandwich
67. spots — leopard
68. headline — newspaper
69. beads — necklace
70. lid — box (pan)
71. door — room
72. sleeve — coat
73. inch — foot
74. wing — bird (plane)
75. zipper — pants

List 70: Level II

Part — Whole	Part — Whole
1. fin — fish	39. skull — skeleton
2. nostril — nose	40. dessert — dinner
3. lobe — ear	41. wristband — watch
4. planets — solar system	42. faucet — sink
5. antenna — television	43. core — apple
6. oar — rowboat	44. seconds — minute
7. trunk — elephant	45. drawbridge — castle
8. bark — tree	46. wishbone — turkey
9. shell — turtle (egg)	47. quills — porcupine
10. exit — store	48. bow — violin
11. fuse — firecracker	49. stripes — tiger (flag)
12. knuckle — finger	50. pupil — class (eye)
13. barrel — gun	51. periscope — submarine
14. index — book	52. inning — baseball game
15. bristles — toothbrush	53. joker — card deck
16. speedometer — car	54. shutter — camera
17. venom — snake	55. December — year (winter)
18. tread — tire	56. dates — calendar
19. rudder — boat	57. brake — car
20. lenses — glasses	58. peak — mountain
21. strings — banjo (guitar)	59. tray — high chair
22. sole — shoe (boot)	60. eraser — pencil
23. rungs — ladder	61. caboose — train
24. wick — candle	62. bars — prison (zoo)
25. speakers — stereo	63. notes — music
26. husk — corn	64. tusk — walrus (elephant)
27. anchor — ship	65. altar — church
28. pincers — crab	66. rind — lemon
29. mane — lion (horse)	67. receiver — telephone
30. flippers — seal	68. trigger — gun
31. cheese — pizza	69. cushion — couch
32. hump — camel	70. angle — triangle
33. buckle — belt	71. hose — vacuum cleaner
34. horse — merry-go-round	72. ruffle — dress
35. hose — gas pump	73. ounce — pound
36. title — book	74. pork chop — pig
37. vault — bank	75. sap — tree
38. label — record (can)	

Lists 71–73: Associations

OBJECTIVE

To develop the student's ability to reason and tell how words are associated and to give divergent and convergent responses.

APPLICATIONS

- Have the students tell why the words go together. Then give one word and have students brainstorm all words associated with it and why they belong (see Level III). Write the words on a chart or have the students make word collages (see illustration on List 73).

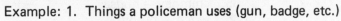

Bride   Groom

- Have the students classify words from the chart or collage in several ways:

    Example: 1. Things a policeman uses (gun, badge, etc.)

    2. Places he might go (court, jail)

    3. Things he does (help, arrest)

- *Association Game*
Place twelve pictures on the table in three rows. The first student covers two pictures with chips and tells how they are related. Second student (or specialist) covers one more and tells how it is associated with the last item covered, and so on. Real objects may be used instead of pictures.

    Example: *Bear* goes with *cat* because they both have fur.

    Cat goes with *tree* because cats climb trees.

    Tree goes with *table* because a table is made from wood from a tree.

- Refer to List 82, Sports, and List 83, Occupations, for other associations.

- Make up sets of real objects for a Go-Together game (candle and holder, flashlight and battery, key and ring). Student finds associated objects and tells *why* they go together.

List 71: Level I

1. chalk — board
2. pencil — paper
3. glove — hand
4. table — chair
5. toothpaste — toothbrush
6. piggy bank — coins
7. ice cream — cone
8. mattress — sheet
9. mouse — cheese
10. tennis ball — racquet
11. stove — pan
12. shoe — shoelace
13. bird — nest
14. hanger — coat
15. ring — finger
16. key — lock
17. baseball — bat
18. pillow — bed
19. stamp — letter
20. flower — vase
21. mop — pail
22. hammer — nail
23. wallet — money
24. stroller — baby
25. drum — sticks
26. fireplace — logs
27. typewriter — paper
28. horse — saddle

29. canoe — paddle
30. puppet — hand
31. stereo — record
32. gun — bullets
33. Christmas tree — decorations
34. cash register — money
35. baby — bottle
36. school — teacher
37. umbrella — rain
38. kite — string
39. sock — shoe
40. paint — brush
41. lawnmower — grass
42. tissues — nose
43. reindeer — Santa Claus
44. license plate — car
45. knitting needles — yarn
46. girl — jacks
47. lamp — light bulb
48. pig — oink
49. cereal — bowl
50. basketball — hoop
51. train — track
52. fork — knife
53. hat — head
54. earphones — ears
55. boat — lake
56. plant — pot
57. suitcase — clothes
58. cow — moo
59. hotdog — bun
60. washing machine — clothes
61. comb — brush
62. bread — butter
63. salt — pepper
64. thunder — lightning

65. gun — holster
66. car — gas
67. fish — hook
68. arrow — bow
69. letter — envelope
70. tire — car
71. car — garage
72. window — curtains
73. sewing machine — cloth
74. whale — ocean
75. bird — cage
76. mailbox — letters
77. Halloween — costumes
78. Goldilocks — Three Bears
79. owl — hoot
80. photographer — camera
81. boxing — gloves
82. sun — heat
83. castle — king
84. balloon — air
85. chimney — house
86. witch — broom
87. spider — web
88. bride — groom
89. coloring book — crayons
90. camera — film
91. lion — roar
92. deer — fawn
93. 4th of July — firecrackers
94. cash register — money
95. fire — heat
96. cow — milk
97. lipstick — lips
98. woodpecker — tree
99. tree — leaves
100. sneeze — cold

List 72: Level II

1. pancake — spatula
2. hockey stick — puck
3. rod — reel
4. airplane — fuel
5. observatory — telescope
6. slide — projector
7. pitchfork — hay
8. quarterback — football
9. carton — milk
10. prison — criminals
11. ax — wood
12. spurs — boots
13. whiskers — razor
14. dice — game
15. tutu — ballet
16. pipe — tobacco
17. mare — foal
18. scale — weight
19. cactus — desert
20. telescope — stars
21. album — photo
22. caterpillar — cocoon
23. gorilla — jungle
24. silo — barn
25. pirate — treasure
26. airplane — parachute
27. hourglass — time
28. encyclopedia — information
29. veins — blood
30. pattern — material
31. fingers — pinch
32. heart — pump
33. violin — concert
34. spring — flowers
35. galoshes — rain
36. yeast — bread
37. exercise — health
38. crosswalk — safety
39. microscope — laboratory
40. chemicals — test tubes
41. moon — tide
42. wand — magician
43. Big Bird — Sesame Street
44. waist — belt
45. diving board — swimming pool
46. stomach — digestion
47. touchdown — football
48. king — knight
49. *Monopoly* — Go!
50. bandage — wound
51. sleigh — horse
52. earthquake — destruction
53. chord — music
54. igloo — Eskimo
55. ghost — Halloween
56. polliwog — frog
57. tongue — swallow
58. pharmacist — pills
59. lighthouse — ship
60. hero — medal
61. bee — wax
62. yarn — sweater
63. pickle — cucumber
64. bat — cave
65. cow — ice cream
66. eraser — mistake
67. contest — award
68. plane — wood
69. block — city
70. hangar — plane
71. turtle — egg
72. horseshoe — hoof
73. starve — thin
74. yardstick — height
75. spy — disguise
76. tank — war
77. cement mixer — building
78. easel — painting
79. spout — whale
80. compass — forest ranger
81. beans — pod
82. cricket — chirp
83. kangaroo — Australia
84. leaves — fall
85. jogging — fatigue
86. apples — vinegar
87. sugar — syrup
88. sand — glass
89. bookworm — reading
90. manicure — fingers
91. checkbook — bills
92. chorus — music
93. surrender — war
94. perspiration — exercise
95. harbor — pier
96. judge — jury
97. politician — campaign
98. artist — studio
99. bricklayer — trowel
100. cabbage — sauerkraut

List 73: Level III Brainstorming

Things associated with *police*

badge	billy club
gun	mace
arrest	radio
help	squad car
uniform	station
blue	protect
motorcycle	rescue
search	whistle
court	investigation
police car	detective
accident	holster
speeding	first aid kit
burglars	tickets
traffic	jail
flares	TV shows
sergeant	

Things associated with *eyes*

glasses	face	telescope
pupil	blue	microscope
stare	camera	monacle
contact lens	blink	opera glasses
blind	eyelids	surgery
sunglasses	sleep	braille
watch	eyedrops	eye shadow
squint	cataract	goggles
wink	crow's feet	cornea
eyelashes	muscles	lens
mascara	binoculars	mirage
color blind	eye doctor	illusion
eye chart	examination	blindfold
sight	patch	focus
black eye	glare	

Other subjects:

cold	Christmas	sharks
muscles	vacations	cavemen
pirates	insects	pollution
bread	hot-air balloons	photography
money	swimming pool	volcanoes

Use subjects from curriculum study topics or current interests and events to make the task more relevant. Have the students make lists at home with family contributions.

Lists 74–75: Similarities/Differences

OBJECTIVE

To develop the student's ability to compare and contrast characteristics of items.

APPLICATIONS

- Prepare a clue chart (see illustration) to assist the student to talk about:

    size, shape, use, location (where it is found), color, parts, sound, texture, material, category.

- Give the student a pair of words from the list orally or on a card. He tells all the ways the items are alike or the ways they are different using clues from the clue chart.

- Use real objects or small toys for the same activity.

List 74: Level I

1. bracelet — necklace
2. orange — grapefruit
3. tape — glue
4. skull — skeleton
5. pin — needle
6. hoe — rake
7. meow — bark
8. bunny — teddy bear
9. tent — trailer
10. gloves — mittens
11. taste — talk
12. butterfly — bird
13. hour — minute
14. bread — biscuit
15. fingers — toes
16. wire — string
17. racquet — bat
18. prison — zoo
19. gun — sword
20. baby — teenager
21. tennis ball — basketball
22. rain — snow
23. bus — train
24. screwdriver — hammer
25. hamburger — hotdog
26. comic book — coloring book
27. staple — paper clip
28. penny — nickel
29. balloon — whistle
30. ladder — stairs
31. magazine — newspaper
32. sled — ski
33. lamp — flashlight
34. jar — can
35. broom — mop
36. typewriter — piano
37. marble — golf ball
38. zebra — horse
39. boat — raft
40. saw — knife
41. bib — napkin
42. button — zipper
43. milk — orange juice
44. worm — snake
45. bed — couch
46. soap — toothpaste
47. stove — refrigerator
48. breakfast — dinner
49. sun — moon
50. wagon — sled
51. chalk — pencil
52. mug — glass
53. ring — glove
54. teacher — principal
55. duck — chicken
56. lion — tiger
57. ambulance — police car
58. motorcycle — bicycle
59. pancake — cupcake
60. jello — pudding
61. house — garage
62. pillow — mattress
63. day — month
64. tree — bush
65. nail — thumbtack
66. president — king

67. lake — ocean
68. whale — shark
69. comb — brush
70. pen — pencil
71. ice cream — popsicle

72. train track — highway
73. painting — drawing
74. summer — winter
75. square — triangle

List 75: Level II

1. pork chop — steak
2. sip — gulp
3. paragraph — chapter
4. sneeze — cough
5. suitcase — trunk
6. wool — satin
7. cockroach — spider
8. trumpet — trombone
9. caboose — engine
10. raccoon — panda
11. Mars — Earth
12. sundial — hourglass
13. telegram — telephone call
14. glider — airplane
15. Private — General
16. polka dots — checks
17. circus — carnival
18. foot — yard
19. spring — summer
20. canal — river
21. spaghetti — macaroni
22. adjective — adverb
23. catalog — dictionary
24. tower — dungeon
25. diamond — ruby
26. periscope — snorkel
27. aircraft carrier — submarine
28. eagle — canary
29. cottage — mansion
30. rose — daisy
31. pitcher — quarterback
32. dictionary — encyclopedia
33. thermometer — speedometer
34. guitar — violin
35. poster — photograph
36. lettuce — cabbage
37. postcard — letter
38. collar — necklace

39. helmet — crown
40. dollar — check
41. dentist — physician
42. umpire — referee
43. waiter — chef
44. zookeeper — veterinarian
45. Rhode Island — California
46. rhinoceros — hippopotamus
47. horse — donkey
48. peach — pear
49. Christmas — Easter
50. ankle — wrist
51. lungs — stomach
52. excited — anxious
53. sight — hearing
54. Sunday — January
55. mountain — hill
56. carrot — potato
57. crib — cradle
58. airplane — rocket
59. crutch — cane
60. elevator — escalator
61. golf club — hockey stick
62. drapes — curtains
63. jackknife — ax
64. minister — rabbi
65. calendar — watch
66. squirrel — chipmunk
67. octopus — squid
68. cantaloupe — watermelon
69. vacation — recess
70. manuscript — cursive
71. deer — moose
72. tornado — hurricane
73. orchestra — band
74. owl — bat
75. carrot — radish

Lists 76-77: Absurd Sentences

OBJECTIVE

To develop the student's ability to analyze sentences presented orally, determine what is absurd and why, and indicate how they can be corrected.

APPLICATIONS

- Read the sentence. Student should identify the error word and correct it. He should tell why the meaning is absurd.

- Have the students make up their own sentences, or use stories they have written and supply incorrect words.

- Refer to List 43, Incomplete Sentences, and List 2, Rhyming Sentences, for similar activities. Supply an incorrect word for the missing one.

The chef booked the spaghetti.

List 76: Absurd Sentences

1.	I smell with my *ear.*	nose
2.	Linda went to the *butcher* shop to get her hair cut.	beauty
3.	I eat ice cream with a *shovel.*	spoon
4.	The *bear* bought a cake at the bakery.	boy
5.	You should brush your *feet* after every meal.	teeth
6.	We went to the *mountain* to go surfboarding.	ocean
7.	California is the nicest *country* in the United States.	state
8.	Do you like to eat baked *beams?*	beans
9.	I eat *stick* and french fries.	steak
10.	I *rod* my bicycle to school.	rode/ride
11.	The hen loves her baby *duckling.*	chick
12.	Did you finish your home *walk?*	work
13.	The *dare* ran through the forest.	deer/bear
14.	The *shop* sailed out to sea.	ship
15.	My sweater has a *hall* in it.	hole
16.	The elephant *drinks* peanuts.	eats
17.	When I am sad, I *laugh* a lot.	cry
18.	*Spoons* bloom in the spring.	flowers
19.	The basement is *up* these stairs.	down
20.	When I go swimming, I get all *dry.*	wet

Absurd Sentences (continued)

21. The piano has 88 *legs*.   keys
22. My *dog* talks a lot on the telephone.   sister/dad
23. My dog has soft *feathers*.   fur
24. When it's dark, we turn *off* the light.   on
25. The grasshopper *crawled* over the fence.   hopped
26. A cowboy rides a *pig*.   horse
27. Ben likes to *fry* his trumpet.   play
28. I use a recipe when I *swim*.   cook
29. My cat has *three* big eyes.   two
30. I take beautiful *words* with my camera.   pictures
31. The sun shines brightly every *night*.   day
32. The horse *hopped* down the road.   trotted
33. Dad winked his *ear* at me.   eye
34. Remember to wind your *witch*.   watch
35. The telephone is *leaking*.   ringing
36. Auntie sat on her favorite *cactus*.   chair
37. Which *telephone* program will you watch?   television
38. The alarm rang at *thirteen* o'clock.   twelve
39. Close the *gate;* I'm cold.   door
40. I told you to vacuum the *ceiling*.   floor
41. Pat put on her *shoes* and went swimming.   suit
42. My brother is *sack* with the measles.   sick
43. We carved a jack-o-lantern for *Christmas*.   Halloween
44. *Beak* the drum loudly.   beat
45. Jack got some new *skis* for ice skating.   skates
46. The giraffe's neck is so *short*.   long
47. Would you like to eat a hamburger or a *coke*?   hot dog
48. The boy dived *on* the diving board.   off
49. Window screens keep the *elephants* out.   flies

List 77: Absurd Sentences with Rhyming Words

1. Mary went for a *talk* on the desert.   walk
2. Did you water your *chant?*   plant
3. The shark *drank* the boat.   sank
4. The monkey *treats* bananas.   eats
5. The light is very *tight.*   bright
6. The lumberjack chopped down a big *bee.*   tree
7. Can you *pray* Monopoly with me?   play
8. I like *belly* on my toast.   jelly
9. I found your number in the telephone *cook.*   book
10. Robin crossed the ocean on a *note.*   boat
11. The airplane flew under the *crowds.*   clouds
12. Dogs love to *marry* bones.   bury
13. Let's all *slow* to the movie.   go
14. Everybody loves *rice* cream.   ice
15. Put your *sungrasses* on when you go outside.   sunglasses
16. The chef *booked* the spaghetti.   cooked
17. The birds *ring* pretty songs.   sing
18. My mother wears a diamond *king.*   ring
19. Susie uses *hope* to wash her clothes.   soap
20. The *pan* blew cool air on us.   fan
21. I like to *feed* books.   read
22. My grandmother sits in a rocking *pear.*   chair
23. The cat chases *rice.*   mice
24. A candle is made of *sacks.*   wax
25. Wine is made from *drapes.*   grapes
26. Greg's teeth are very *late.*   straight
27. The baby drinks from his *throttle.*   bottle
28. A Ford is a kind of *star.*   car
29. The man *threw* his nose.   blew
30. John wears a *felt* with his jeans.   belt
31. Sally bought a new *mess* today.   dress
32. A dentist uses a *grill.*   drill
33. Tom wore a suit and *cry* to the wedding.   tie
34. Your dog was once a *guppy.*   puppy
35. Jack *rowed* the lawn.   mowed
36. The *carrot* is in his cage.   parrot

37. John plays his trumpet in the *sand*.   band

38. I bought a candy bar with my *pickle*.   nickel

39. The mother bird *blew* to her nest.   flew

40. Put on your *goat* when you go outside.   coat

41. The cow gives *silk*.   milk

42. The puppy ran down the *load*.   road

43. The man caught a *dish* in the lake.   fish

44. I put a stamp on the *sweater*.   letter

45. The man at the game sold peanuts and hot *frogs*.   hot dogs

46. I tore the sleeve of my *skirt*.   shirt

47. The king is wearing his *clown*.   crown

48. Light the *sandal* so we can see.   candle

49. We painted the *fall* blue.   wall

50. We need a new roof on our *mouse*.   house

Lists 78–79: Inferences (riddles)

OBJECTIVE

To develop the student's ability to combine and use information given to solve problems.

APPLICATIONS

- ◆ Read the first general clue to the riddle. Elicit from the students as many appropriate responses as possible. List them on a chart.

  Read the second clue. Encourage students to combine all information to make a judgment. Have them evaluate each previous answer to see if it fits all clues.

  Read the third clue.

- ◆ Refer to List 43, Incomplete Sentences, and List 2, Rhyming Sentences, for similar context clue activities.

- ◆ Refer to Lists 82 to 87 for subjects for other riddles.

List 78: Level I

1. I am cold and wet.
   I am full of bubbles.
   You drink me when you're hot.   soda pop

2. I wear a big hat.
   I ride on a big truck.
   I use a hose to put out fires.   fireman

3. I taste sweet.
   I am made from flower nectar.
   Bees make me.   honey

4. I live on a farm.
   I am big and eat hay.
   I give milk.   cow

5. I am good to drink.
   I am white.
   I rhyme with silk.   milk

6. Girls use me.
   I come in different shades of red.
   I am worn on the mouth.   lipstick

7. People make things with me.
   Part of me goes up and down very fast.
   I make stitches.   sewing machine

8. I am black and white.
   I am a furry forest animal.
   Sometimes I give off a bad smell.   skunk

9. I am round.
   I am juicy and sweet.
   I am orange in color.   orange

10. I use scissors when I work.
    I work on someone in a big chair.
    I sweep up lots of hair.   barber

11. I often wear a black robe.
    I pound with a gavel.
    I give out sentences in a courtroom.   judge

12. I have a long barrel.
    I am used for hunting.
    Someone pulls my trigger.   rifle

13. I am a big building.
    Lots of people come inside together.
    I am usually used on weekends for services.   church

14. I gather twigs and strings.
    I weave these together to make a home.
    I keep eggs in it.   bird

15. I look at people very carefully.
    I usually see them when they are sick.
    I give out medicine.   doctor

16. I am used to hold things together.
    I come in a bottle or tube.
    I am white and sticky.   glue

17. I am about 10 inches long and thin.
    I am Italian.
    Tomato sauce is poured over me.   spaghetti

18. I am made of metal.
    I have wheels.
    People ride on me.   bicycle

19. I come from a tree.
    I am chopped.
    I am burned in a fireplace.   logs

20. I have a long cord.
    I am connected to speakers.
    I am used to amplify voices.   microphone

21. I am made from wood.
    I clean up spills.
    I am very thin and am kept in the kitchen.   paper towels

22. I get very hot.
    I give off steam.
    I am used to press clothes.   iron

23. I live in the ocean.
    I eat almost anything.
    I have a fin and sharp teeth.   shark

24. I am hunted by men.
    I run fast and have a white tail.
    I have antlers.   deer

25. I am very colorful.
    People like to look at me on a wall.
    I am made by an artist.

    painting

26. I am very soft.
    I have sharp claws and drink milk.
    I like to play with string.

    cat

27. I have two hands.
    I have numbers from one to twelve.
    I measure time.

    clock

28. I am made of glass.
    I use electricity.
    I light up a room.

    light bulb

29. I am long and wooden.
    I am used in a game.
    I am used to hit a ball.

    bat

30. I run very fast.
    I am big and muscular.
    I eat hay and wear a saddle.

    horse

31. I break easily.
    I am white and oval-shaped.
    I have a yolk.

    egg

32. I like water and light.
    I am green.
    I have leaves.

    plant

33. I am part of a house.
    I am made of glass.
    You can see through me.

    window

34. I have numbers on me.
    I make a noise.
    People use me to communicate.

    telephone

35. I have a long string.
    I go up and down.
    I am a toy.

    yoyo

36. I get very hot.
    I melt quickly.
    I am made of wax.

    candle

37. I carry food.
    I take orders.
    I work in a restaurant.

    waiter or waitress

38. I am gold in color.
    I swim all the time.
    I live in a bowl.

    goldfish

39. I am worn on the face.
    I have a frame.
    I help people to see.

    glasses

40. I am a dessert.
    I am eaten on a special day.
    Sometimes I have candles on me.

    birthday cake

41. I am a piece of clothing.
    I am worn over other clothes.
    I am worn in wet weather.   raincoat

42. I am white and furry.
    I have a fluffy tail.
    I eat carrots.   rabbit

43. I am a machine.
    I use gasoline.
    I cut grass.   lawn mower

44. I am a container.
    I am used to hold liquids.
    People drink from me.   glass or cup

45. I am worn by an athlete.
    I am worn where it is cold.
    I have a blade on a shoe.   ice skate

46. I am made of cloth.
    I am put on a flat piece of furniture.
    Plates and silverware are set on me.   tablecloth

47. I am a special woman.
    I can rule a country.
    Sometimes I sit on a throne.   queen

48. I am a kind of ball.
    Two or four people hit me in a game.
    I am hit with paddles.   ping pong ball

49. I am a large vehicle.
    People travel a long way on me.
    I travel on the water.   ship

50. I am an outdoor place.
    Many people gather at me at the same time.
    The people watch a game here.   stadium

List 79: Level II

1. I am a kind of store.
   People come to me when they are sick.
   I have lots of pills.

   drugstore

2. I love to swim.
   I am a very large mammal.
   I spout water from my back.

   whale

3. I have a lot of teeth.
   I help build houses.
   Carpenters use me.

   saw

4. I hang on buildings.
   I am very cold and pointed.
   Sunshine melts me.

   icicle

5. I float above the earth.
   I travel by rocket.
   I wear a special suit.

   astronaut

6. I can crawl or swing through the air.
   I build a special kind of house.
   I have eight legs.

   spider

7. I am long and thin.
   I have numbers on me.
   You put me in your mouth.

   thermometer

8. I am a big building.
   I have towers.
   Kings or rulers live in me.

   castle

9. I really "bug" people.
   I fly and make a noise.
   I sting.

   mosquito

10. I take people places.
    I have rubber tires.
    I have two wheels and a motor.

    motorcycle

11. I answer questions.
    I wear headphones.
    I work at a switchboard.

    telephone operator

12. I scrub floors and wash clothes.
    I once lost a shoe.
    I have a fairy godmother.

    Cinderella

13. I am very big.
    I have a harp and a golden hen.
    I climbed down a beanstalk.

    giant

14. I travel every day.
    I have a door and no windows.
    I take people up and down.

    elevator

15. I am a large vehicle.
    I stop at every house.
    I collect trash.

    garbage truck

16. I am very cold.
    I get smaller every minute.
    People like to eat me in the summertime.

    ice cream cone

17. I am brown and sticky.
    People eat me.
    I'm good with jelly.   peanut butter

18. I bend a lot.
    I am part of the body.
    I'm between your hand and shoulder.   elbow

19. I am in the shape of a rectangle.
    People put me up in the air.
    I have stars and stripes.   flag

20. I am metal and have two handles.
    People put things in me.
    I have one wheel.   wheelbarrow

21. I am white and soft.
    I am square and come in a box.
    You use me for your nose.   tissues

22. I use a whistle when I work.
    I work near the water.
    Sometimes I save people.   lifeguard

23. I am round and heavy.
    People use me in a sport.
    I have three holes and I hit pins.   bowling ball

24. I wear a uniform.
    Sometimes I march in parades.
    I help protect our country.   soldier

25. I am a jungle animal.
    I run fast and am very strong.
    I have stripes.   tiger

26. I am made of cloth and metal.
    People take me on vacations.
    People sleep in me.   tent

27. I am brown and furry.
    I live on the desert.
    I have a large hump on my back.   camel

28. I am grey and live in the forest.
    Most animals leave me alone.
    I am covered with sharp quills.   porcupine

29. I am made of words.
    People recite me.
    I usually rhyme.   poem

30. I am a leader.
    Many people vote for me.
    I live in the White House.   President

31. I am wide at the bottom and pointed on top.
    I am outside and can be very dangerous.
    Smoke and fire come out my top.   volcano

32. I am a famous dog.
    You see me on TV.
    I have a friend named Charlie.   Snoopy

33. I give orders to people.
    I tell them when to stop and go.
    I have three colored lights.   traffic signal

34. I come in different colors and shapes.
    People fill me up.
    I can make a loud pop one time.   balloon

35. I was a famous little girl.
    Someone wrote a story about me.   Little Red
    A big forest animal scared me.   Riding Hood

36. I am a place you have visited.
    People drive to me often.
    I have lots of pumps.   gas station

37. You use me every day.
    You feel me but you can't see me.
    You see me on Valentines.   heart

38. I am a big machine.
    I have a big blade in front.
    I move dirt.   bulldozer

39. I am a leader of a group of people.
    They watch me while they play.
    We all love music.   band leader

40. I am not real.
    Halloween is my favorite night.
    I live in a haunted house.   ghost

List 80: Logical Sequences

OBJECTIVE

To develop the student's ability to order items in logical sequences.

APPLICATIONS

♦ Present a group of words from the list in scrambled order orally or on a card. Start with only three items if four is too difficult.

♦ Ordering one large group such as animals can be a challenging activity. Brainstorm all the names first. Then have students order them by size, etc. Refer to Lists 65 to 68, Classification, for group titles.

♦ Make timelines for the student's life events, sections of history, a school program (what happened first, next), etc.

♦ Order objects or toys according to size, shades of color, weight, sharpness, volume, noise, or other characteristics.

Example: spoons, colored paper, screws or bolts, noisemakers, toy cars, egg carton sections, pencils, etc.

♦ Students may add more items to these groups or make up new groups.

SIZE

neighborhood — city — state — country
tent — cabin — store — skyscraper
mouse — dog — mule — elephant
tadpole — fish — shark — whale
puddle — pond — lake — ocean
ashtray — wastebasket — garbage can — dump
flea — bee — bird — stork
ping pong ball — golf ball — tennis ball — baseball
kitten — cub — colt — hippopotamus
piece of paper — comic book — math book — dictionary
grape — plum — orange — watermelon
rowboat — sailboat — ferry boat — ship
stamp — postcard — magazine — newspaper
grass — flower — bush —tree
inch — foot — yard — mile
word — sentence — paragraph — book
satellite — moon — earth — sun

WEIGHT OR VOLUME

feather — marble — tennis ball — dictionary
pint — quart — ½ gallon — gallon
cup — pail — bathtub — swimming pool
chair — table — piano — car

VALUE

bicycle — motorcycle — car — train
penny — nickel — dime — quarter
5 — 10 — 15 — 20
lampshade — TV set — car — house
grape — orange — loaf of bread — steak
stick — yoyo — baseball — race car set

TIME

January — May — September — December
Monday — Tuesday — Friday — Saturday
breakfast — lunch — dinner — midnight snack
day — week — month — year
New Year's — Easter — 4th of July — Christmas
baby — teenager — father — grandparent
ancient — old — modern — futuristic
last week — yesterday — today — tomorrow

SOUND VOLUME

whisper — talk — yell — scream
peep — meow — growl — roar
flute — trumpet — car horn — siren

LOCATION

toes — leg — knees — thigh
head — neck — shoulders — chest
basement — ground floor — 2nd floor — attic
shoes — pants — shirt — hat

SPEED

skate — bike — helicopter — jet
hop — walk — skip — run
turtle — pig — horse — cheetah

TEMPERATURE

ice cube — jello — bread — chili
icy — cool — warm — boiling
Arizona — Hawaii — Minnesota — Alaska

OTHER

private — sergeant — colonel — general
councilman — mayor — governor — president
match — candle — light bulb — spotlight
undershirt — shirt — jacket — overcoat

V. Production of Language (non-verbal, verbal, written)

A. NON-VERBAL

81. Body language, level I
82. Body language, sports
83. Body language, occupations
84. Body language, emotions and feelings
85. Body language, transportation
86. Body language, locations
87. Sequence of actions

B. VERBAL

88. Production of sentences
89. Descriptive language
90. Story--telling
91. Demonstration talks
92. Mini--talks
93. People talks
94. Commercials and announcements
95. Interview topics
96. Improvisations

List 81: Body Language, Beginning Level

OBJECTIVE

To develop the student's ability to express a simple idea through specific body movements.

APPLICATIONS

* Demonstrate several body pantomimes. Emphasize specific action. Have students watch your face, your hands, your movements.

* Do the simple actions *with* the students. Talk about what you are doing.

  Example: "Pick up the needle. It is very thin. Now try and put the thread through the hole. Carefully! Pull it through to the other side. Now let's tie a knot in the thread."

* If possible, show a picture clue to the student before he does a pantomime. "Remember you are going to tell us what this is without words."

* Let students do pantomimes individually. Give feedback such as "I could really see the trumpet in your hand. You looked like you were blowing hard on it."

* Refer to List 28, Antonyms, and List 23, Homophones, for other simple pantomime subjects.

PANTOMIMES

1. blow your nose
2. wash your hair
3. eat corn on the cob
4. type on typewriter
5. wash your clothes
6. play a violin or trumpet
7. pound a nail with a hammer
8. rake up leaves
9. pour milk and drink it
10. play with a bug in your hand
11. chop down a tree
12. make a peanut butter sandwich
13. feed a dog
14. sharpen a pencil
15. blow up a balloon
16. brush your teeth
17. paint a picture

18. play a pinball machine
19. mow the lawn
20. eat an ice cream cone
21. eat hot soup
22. put on a jacket with a zipper
23. put out a campfire
24. climb a tree
25. open and use an umbrella
26. juggle some balls
27. hold a baby
28. thread a needle
29. paint a wall
30. play cards
31. write a letter
32. use the telephone
33. wash a window
34. replace a light bulb
35. read a newspaper
36. set the dinner table
37. put on cowboy boots
38. open a present
39. play a guitar
40. color in a coloring book
41. eat a popsicle
42. use a tape recorder
43. comb and brush your hair
44. erase the chalkboard
45. mop the floor
46. water your plants
47. use a cash register
48. take a shower
49. get into a sleeping bag
50. wash the dishes

List 82: Body Language, Advanced — Sports

OBJECTIVE

To develop the student's ability to express an emotion or idea through a series of body movements coordinated with facial expressions.

APPLICATIONS

* Let each student draw a card with the *Sport* and *object used* printed on it. He should show how he uses the object as he performs actions associated with that sport. Encourage him to use facial expressions to show mood.

* Make comments such as, "You are telling us with your body what is happening. How do you hold the racquet? Now watch for the ball. Move quickly and hit it. Good! Now what do you do?". Have other students wait until the pantomime is finished before they put up their hands to guess the subject.

    If the student has difficulty getting started, do it with him or let another student join in.

* Do the same with **Occupations** and objects used.

* **Emotions** — Ask students to show you with their *faces* and *bodies* the emotion listed on the card.

* **Forms of Transportation** — Student should pantomime *getting in* or *on* and moving to the other side of the room in the characteristic way.

* **Locations** — Students should show *going in* or *to* the place and what they would do there.

* Give lots of feedback and encouragement and do frequent demonstrations.

* Select items on the vocabulary level of your students.

Sport	Object used
archery	bow and arrow
arm wrestling	table
basketball	hoop
bicycling	bicycle
boxing	gloves
badminton	birdie
bullfighting	cape
baseball	mitt
bowling	pins
billiards	cue
bobsledding	chute
car racing	track

Sport	Object used
croquet	mallet
canoeing	paddle
cricket	wicket
dodgeball	ball
darts	target
diving	diving board
discus throw	measuring tape
football	goal posts
fencing	foils
falconry	glove
fishing	reel
golf	clubs
gymnastics	mat
gliding	plane
hockey	ice
hurdles	track shoes
hang gliding	cliff
horseback riding	saddle
horseshoes	post
hopscotch	rock
hiking	boots
hunting	rifle
ice skating	rink
jump rope	rope
jogging	jogging shoes
judo	robe
jacks	ball
karate	hands
marbles	boulder
motorcycling	helmet
mountain climbing	rope
ping pong	paddle
pole vaulting	bar
pool	cue ball
polo	horses
racquet ball	court
rowing	oar
roller skating	rink
rugby	field
swimming	pool

Sport	Object used
skydiving	parachute
surfing	waves
scuba diving	wet suit
soccer	ball
sailing	mast
shuffleboard	disc
skiing	boots
spearfishing	spear
skin diving	snorkel
speedball	ball
surfboarding	surfboard
tetherball	post
tennis	racquet
tobogganing	toboggan
target shooting	rifle
volleyball	net
wrestling	mat
weight lifting	barbell
water skiing	boat
water polo	ball

List 83: Body Language, Advanced – Occupations

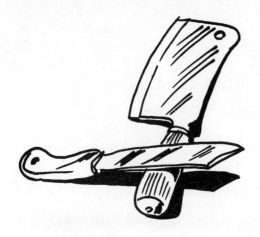

Occupation	Associated object used
announcer	microphone
auctioneer	podium
astronaut	spaceship
accountant	calculator
architect	drawing board
animal trainer	whip
archaeologist	pick
artist	palette
actor	script
astronomer	telescope
bus driver	license
barber	scissors
baseball player	glove
bricklayer	trowel
botanist	microscope
biographer	typewriter
butcher	cleaver
blacksmith	anvil
boxer	gloves
baker	pans
banker	vault
bookkeeper	record books
chemist	test tubes
cartoonist	pens
carpet layer	glue
custodian	mop
carpenter	hammer
construction worker	hard hat
chef	pots and pans
clown	makeup
coach	stopwatch

Occupation	Associated object used
checker	scale
cement worker	cement mixer
dishwasher	dish racks
dressmaker	sewing machine
dancer	leotard
doctor	stethoscope
dentist	drill
dietician	menus
drafter	drawing table
detective	magnifying glass
dog groomer	shears
engineer	calculator
farmer	plow
forest ranger	binoculars
florist	tape
firefighter	hose
furniture mover	dolly
fisher	net
flight attendant	food trays
gardener	lawnmower
grocer	cash register
geologist	geiger counter
glass blower	fire
hairdresser	blow dryer
homemaker	stove
judge	gavel
juggler	pins
king	crown
lifeguard	whistle
librarian	card catalog
lawyer	law books

Occupation	Associated object used
lumberjack	axe
linesman (telephone)	cable
mail carrier	bags
miner	pick
musician	instrument
mechanic	wrench
model	runway
mathematician	calculator
minister	prayer book
magician	wand
maid	feather duster
nurse	thermometer
opera singer	stage
optometrist	eye chart
painter	overalls
pizza maker	rolling pin
printer	press
plumber	pipe wrench
police officer	gun
physical therapist	parallel bars
politician	speeches
potter	clay
pharmacist	scales
photographer	tripod
piano tuner	tuning fork
psychologist	IQ tests
publisher	contract
producer (TV)	monitors
paper carrier	rubber bands

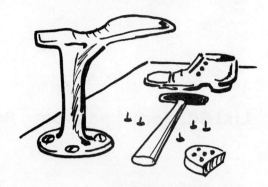

Occupation	Associated object used
pilot	instruments
rabbi	holy book
reporter	tape recorder
referee	whistle
rancher	cattle
railroad engineer	switches
roofer	shingles
sailor	rope
salesperson	receipts
soldier	rifle
service station operator	gas pump
scientist	laboratory
surveyor	telescope
secretary	telephone
surgeon	scalpel
sky diver	parachute
sculptor	chisel
shoemaker	leather
singer	sheet music
switchboard operator	earphones
sign painter	stencils
camera operator (TV)	dolly, boom
truck driver	CB radio
teacher	chalkboard
tailor	pattern
TV technician	screwdriver
tourist guide	guidebooks
translator	dictionary
ticket seller	cage
umpire	face guard
usher	flashlight
veterinarian	examining table
ventriloquist	dummy
waiter or waitress	order pad
watch repairman	eyeglass
welder	welding torch
weather forecaster	barometer
zookeeper	cages

List 84: Body Language, Advanced—Emotions and Feelings

ashamed	ill
achy	interested
afraid	innocent
angry	irritated
amazed	inquisitive
astounded	itchy
amused	joyful
alert	jumpy
annoyed	lonely
attentive	lively
anxious	mad
bored	mixed-up
bewildered	nervous
brave	overjoyed
cold	overwhelmed
curious	puzzled
calm	proud
confused	pained
cheerful	panicky
disgusted	pleased
disappointed	relaxed
delighted	reverent
doubtful	relieved
depressed	sad
defiant	sleepy
entranced	shocked
eager	sorrowful
excited	sick
energetic	scared
envious	silly
enthusiastic	surprised
embarrassed	strong
exhausted	troubled
elated	tired
frightened	tickled
fascinated	tense
friendly	timid
furious	thankful
fidgety	thirsty
foolish	unfriendly
frantic	uptight
guilty	victorious
grieving	vivacious
happy	worried
hungry	weary
hopeful	wicked
haughty	weak
hurt	

List 85: Body Language, Advanced — Transportation

ambulance
airplane
bicycle
baby buggy
bus
bucket lift (used by
    telephone repairmen)
barge
camel
covered wagon
car
canoe
catamaran
cannon (human cannonball)
conveyor belt
creeper (used by mechanics)
caterpillar (tractor)
dogsled
donkey
diving bell
dump truck
elephant
escalator
elevator
fire engine
gondola
glider
golf cart
go-cart
helicopter
hydrofoil
horse
hot air balloon
hang glider
houseboat
inner tube (for river floating)
ice skates
jet
kayak
litter (for patients)
merry-go-round
magic carpet
monorail
moped
mobile home
ostrich
parachute
pogo stick

rowboat
roller coaster
raft
rickshaw
rocketship
racer
stretcher
sleigh
ski-lift
speedboat
skateboard
sled
skis
submarine
stroller
ship
sailboat
surrey
snowmobile
stagecoach
shopping cart (children)
street sweeper
scooter
stilts
tractor
tram
tricycle
train
tugboat
tank
trapeze
unicycle
vine (Tarzan)
wagon
water skis
wheelchair
yacht
zeppelin

List 86: Body Language, Advanced— Locations

in an apple tree
on an aircraft carrier
in an avalanche
in a blizzard
on the beach
on the back of a bucking bronco
at a birthday party
at a bank holdup
in a burning building
in a beauty shop
at church
in a computer center
in a locked closet
in a courtroom
by a campfire
at a used car lot
in a canoe
at a car accident
at a circus
in a dark cave
at a card party
on a dry desert
on a high diving board
in a doughnut factory
in a duststorm
in a darkroom
in a dance studio
in a dentist's office
in a disco
on the edge of a cliff
in an elevator
on an escalator
at the eye doctor's office

in an emergency room
in a fire station
at a football game
in a furniture store
in a fishbowl
in a gold mine
at a garbage dump
in a gym
on a hayride
in a hospital bed in traction
on a hang glider
in a helicopter
in a deep hole
at a hotel
on a deserted island
in an igloo
in an ice cream parlour
in a jewelry store
in jail
in a jungle
in a kitchen
in a library
in a magic lamp (a genie)
in a mouse hole
at an art museum
on a mountain top
at a movie
on the moon
in a monster's mouth
at a movie studio
in a baby nursery
at a plant nursery
at an opera
in an observatory
in a photographic studio
at the police station
in a parade
on a picnic
in a pet shop
at a masquerade party
on the playground
in quicksand
at a riding stable

on a raft
on a roof
in a restaurant
at a record store
at a service station
on a slide
on a swing
on a ship in a storm
at a shoe store
on a ski slope
in a sea lab
at the State Fair
in the shower
at the Statue of Liberty
in a treehouse

in a theatre
on a trapeze
at a TV game show
in a taxi
in a ticket booth
on a train
on a tightrope
at a tennis game
in a telephone booth
on top of a telephone pole
on a truck loading dock
in a toy store
on a unicycle
at a wedding
in a telephone booth

List 87: Sequence of Actions

OBJECTIVE

To develop the student's ability to demonstrate a series of sequential ideas through body movements alone and with verbalization.

APPLICATIONS

+ "You are going to tell us a story without words. Think about each part of the story. Show us *where* you are and *what* you are doing."

+ Student draws a slip of paper with the sequence printed on it. Give him a few minutes to plan. Then he acts it out. Sidecoach if necessary as in the simple pantomimes, List 81. Perhaps let the student pick a *hat* to wear to help him get into character.

+ Let another student explain the sequence he saw performed. Talk about what you saw.

+ If possible, video tape the sequence and replay it for evaluation.

+ These activities may also be used with verbalizing.

+ Refer to Lists 41 and 42, Scrambled Sentence Sequence, for other ideas.

1. Put a saddle on a horse.
   Get on.
   Try to make him go.
   He won't go.

2. Fill a glass with water from the faucet.
   Start to drink.
   Someone sneaks up behind and scares you.
   Drop the glass.

3. You are digging with a pick.
   Find a box.
   Open it and find a ring.
   Put it on.

4. Use a pair of binoculars.
   See something fantastic.
   Run to a friend and tell him about it.

5. Wake up.
   Smell smoke.
   Look for a fire.
   Find a fire in the kitchen.

6. Cut a piece of cake.
   Start to eat.
   Bite on something hard and break your tooth.
   Show pain.

7. Make a paper airplane.
   Throw it.
   It hits someone.
   Apologize.

8. You are playing the piano.
   Make a mistake.
   Keep trying to do it right.
   Finally give up and walk out.

9. You are sneaking a cookie from the cookie jar.
   Your mom surprises you by opening the door.
   Show your reaction.

10. Get in a taxi.
    Tell the driver where you want to go.
    After the ride you think he charged you too much.

11. Someone calls you on the telephone.
    Listen carefully.
    You've won a fantastic prize!

12. Go out to take a sunbath.
    Put lotion on.
    Lie down and get comfortable.
    You feel a raindrop, then a cloudburst.

13. Answer the doorbell.
    The mailman has a big package for you.
    Open it excitedly. It is just a _____.

14. Pick out something to buy at the store.
    Start to pay for it.
    Find out your money is missing.
    Look for it frantically.

15. You are fishing.
    You feel something on the line.
    Reel it in with a struggle.
    It is just an old tire.

16. You are walking to school.
    You hear or see a car accident.
    Run over and help someone.

17. Open the door to your gerbil or mouse cage to feed your pet.
    He gets out.
    Chase him and try to find him.

18. Eat an ice cream cone.
    A bee lands on it.
    Try to get him away.
    Finally drop your cone.

19. Watch television.
    The show is very exciting.
    Suddenly the TV set stops working.
    Try to fix it.
    Give up.

20. You are in the forest throwing crumbs to squirrels.
    You hear something.
    Look! It's a bear!
    Try to leave without him hearing you.

List 88: Production of Sentences

The grey cat... ..um,...ran into the house.

OBJECTIVE

To develop the student's ability to compose complete and meaningful sentences when given word cues.

APPLICATIONS

- Give the student a three–word group from the list with or without a visual cue. The student makes up a sentence using the words in any order.
- The student may make up a second sentence that would logically follow the first one.
- Let the student select two objects from a box and make up a sentence about them. Pictures may also be used.
- To improve the production of compound and complex sentences, see the second activity at the end of List 88.

1. lion — cage — growls
2. fish — many — ocean
3. car — small — fast
4. hard — work — tired
5. boat — wind — blew
6. waves — shore — seaweed
7. lady — smiles — dog
8. Goldilocks — chair — porridge
9. Red Riding Hood — wolf — woods
10. airplane — passengers — frightened
11. baby — cried — wet
12. Snow White — prince — kissed
13. spaceship — flew — moon
14. Peter Rabbit — garden — carrots
15. maid — apron — works
16. little — walks — child
17. alligator — swamp — green
18. Gingerbread Man — oven — ran
19. Dumbo — flew — ears
20. soup — Bobby — bowl
21. whistle — coach — race
22. Humpty Dumpty — wall — cracked
23. Miss Muffet — spider — scared
24. night — roller coaster — scary
25. white — waitress — dress
26. hot dogs — hamburger — Jean
27. Wednesday — birthday — Jack
28. arm — skateboard — riding
29. barn — cow — fence

30. raccoon — cat — milk
31. car — windshield — accident
32. Bo–Peep — sheep — lost
33. Winnie-the-Pooh — stuck —hole
34. Snoopy — doghouse — sleeps
35. clown — monkey — circus
36. autumn — pumpkins — jack-o-lanterns
37. President — vote — November
38. motorcycle — street — doctor
39. duck — turkey— farmer
40. soldier — jeep — mountains
41. noise — drum — music
42. milkshake — McDonalds — night
43. storm — tree — river
44. scarecrow — birds — fence
45. laughing — Paul — movie
46. sneezed — hat — Brenda
47. Jean — fudge — stove
48. ring — wedding — bride
49. witch — broom — sky
50. Bambi — born — forest
51. Cinderella — lost — midnight
52. wolf — house — blew
53. Sleeping Beauty — years — slept
54. Disneyland — vacation — family
55. baseball — fence — Brian
56. ocean — whales — grey
57. sharks — swimmers — careful
58. wild — jungle — trees
59. wood — giant — chopped
60. skeletons — house — bones
61. Bobby — peanuts — twenty
62. bird — nest — tree
63. Troll — billy-goat — bridge
64. Popeye — spinach — strong
65. Bugs Bunny — carrots — day
66. dive — board — swimming pool
67. fireman — rescued — building
68. judge — burglar — jail
69. hen — eggs — nest
70. Paul — report card — dad
71. Santa Claus — reindeer — sleigh
72. yoyo — new — store
73. baseball — home run — Cindy
74. spider — web — woodpile
75. football — stadium — crowd

Production of Sentences (continued)

Read to the student the sentence beginning or have him read it from a card. He draws a word card with one of the following words on it:

during
after
and
when
but
because
before
while

Then he finishes the sentence using that word. The next student may draw another card and use the same sentence beginning.

Example: The lion roared (because he was hungry).
(after he ate dinner).
(while he was eating).

1. The lion roared _____.

2. The ghost appeared _____.

3. The quarterback threw the ball _____.

4. The President gave a speech _____.

5. I called my mom _____.

6. Julie found $100 _____.

7. The scouts discovered a cave _____.

8. The clown did a somersault _____.

9. We went on a roller coaster _____.

10. The police chased the robber _____.

11. The cars crashed _____.

12. We went to the circus _____.

13. You can eat your candy bar _____.

14. Cinderella lost her shoe _____.

15. Billy got the measles _____.

16. Snoopy sat on his doghouse _____.

17. I like to play baseball _____.

18. The monkey climbed the tree _____.

19. My little brother cried _____.

20. We will go to the zoo _____.

List 89: Descriptive Language

OBJECTIVE

To develop the student's ability to give descriptions and directions verbally using precise language to convey meaning.

APPLICATIONS

- **Giving Directions**
  Provide the students with or have them draw a simple map of the school area, neighborhood, city, state or country. Encourage them to use directional terms such as north, east, left, diagonally, parallel, etc. as they give directions. Try to elicit very *specific* language.

- **Descriptions**
  Put some interesting objects on a table. Let the student select one and give a talk describing every aspect of the object. The students may also describe another student in detail.

- Show a story filmstrip with narration. Then have the student narrate using descriptive language. Tape record his version and play back for evaluation.

- Have the students give travelogues using slides from home or school or pictures from travel magazines.

- Refer to List 91, Demonstration Talks, for a related activity.

Give Directions to Find:

1. the nearest fire station
2. the principal's office
3. Disneyland
4. the flagpole
5. the baseball diamond
6. your house
7. the nearest park
8. your favorite eating place
9. the zoo
10. the nearest theatre
11. the Statue of Liberty
12. the nearest grocery store
13. the library
14. hospital or nurse's office
15. the drinking fountain
16. a nearby state or city
17. the nearest gas station
18. the cafeteria
19. a bus stop
20. the nearest body of water
21. points of interest in your city or state
22. other countries
23. national parks
24. China
25. the North Pole
26. the pencil sharpener
27. Washington, D. C.
28. Mexico

Describe in Detail:

1. an alligator
2. your bedroom
3. the library
4. one of your family
5. a rose
6. your right foot
7. the wastebasket
8. the American flag
9. an ice cream cone
10. the principal or another teacher
11. a walrus
12. an airplane
13. a typewriter
14. George Washington
15. the drinking fountain
16. Frankenstein
17. the moon
18. your school
19. Mickey Mouse
20. a shark

List 90: Story-Telling

OBJECTIVE

To develop the student's ability to spontaneously create and verbalize a sequence of events through story-telling.

APPLICATIONS

• **Story Openers**

Read a story to the students using a lot of animation in voice and character or play a good story record. Talk about how to make a story exciting.

• Read a "Story Opener." The student continues the story until a signal is given. Other students or the clinician then continue, and so on. Encourage colorful language and lively voice inflection. Record the stories. They may be played back for evaluation and also for parents to enjoy.

• **Shape Stories**

Let the students dictate stories to you or to a tape recorder. Print or type the stories on construction paper shapes (balloon, television set, boat, animal, violin, etc.). Save the stories and make them into books to be sent home later for the families to enjoy. See Appendix for shape patterns.

• Use these stories for improvisation.

• **Story-Telling**

The students may practice telling short versions of fairy tales for improvement in projection, inflection, sentence construction and eye contact. Visual aids may be used such as flannel boards, puppets, etc. Refer to Lists 99 and 100 for story suggestions.

1. One morning there was a little brown furry bunny on my doorstep and _____.

2. My uncle gave me a ride in his hot-air balloon and _____.

3. One night I walked into a dark haunted house and _____.

4. I dreamed that I was given a million dollars and _____.

5. I got a big box in the mail and inside it was _____.

6. One day I got an exciting long distance telephone call and _____.

7. When I was walking through a dark cave, I met a _____.

8. One time I was baking a new cake recipe. I looked in the oven and to my surprise I saw _____.

9. Once I dreamed my stuffed animals could talk to me. My teddy bear told me _____.

10. Once I was on a TV game show and I _____.

11. One morning I woke up and I found out I had turned into a little mouse and _____.

12. One day I ate some spinach. My muscles started growing and I became super strong. Then I _____.

13. Once I was on a boat and I got lost. I landed on a deserted island and _____.

14. I was running really fast one day and all of a sudden I started to fly. I _____.

15. Once I climbed up a tree and found a nest. Inside of it was _____.

16. One time I went deep sea diving and I discovered _____.

17. I dreamed I was Queen of England and every day I could _____.

18. I was one of the first humans to live in a space colony. For fun we _____.

19. One day I invented a robot and the best thing about it was _____.

20. I got a magic pony for Christmas. I got on his back and we _____.

21. One time I went to a fortune teller. She told me that _____.

22. I made a new friend yesterday. He wasn't an ordinary friend. He was _____.

23. On April Fool's Day my little brother played the world's biggest trick on me. He _____.

24. I went up in a rocketship with an astronaut. We were flying through space and _____.

25. When I was running through the woods one day, I fell into a pool of water and went through to a different world. It was _____.

26. Once I was hunting for peacocks in the jungle. Suddenly I found I was being chased by _____.

27. One day I was climbing a tree. All of a sudden the sky turned dark and I saw a tornado coming. It _____.

28. One day I locked myself out of the house. I was okay until _____.

29. I was working in an ice cream parlor. One day I started to make the biggest sundae in the world. It _____.

30. I dreamed I was a sheriff tracing down some desperadoes. I got on my horse and _____.

31. One night there was a thunderstorm and all the lights went out. My dog and I were alone. We heard _____.

32. I dreamed I was a scientist. I made a special potion and when I drank it _____.

33. Once I fell asleep for twenty years. When I woke up I found that _____.

34. Once I had a magic violin. When I played the right note _____.

35. I was on the beach looking for shells. I saw an old man who told me _____.

36. Last year my hometown had a huge parade just for me because I _____.

Lists 91–92: Demonstration Talks and Mini-Talks

A. DEMONSTRATION TALKS

OBJECTIVE

To develop the student's ability to describe orally the sequential steps in a process and to use visual aids.

APPLICATIONS

- Encourage students to use objects, charts, drawings or other visual aids.

  Emphasize the *sequence of activities* in the demonstration talks. Have other students listen carefully and remember any steps missed in the sequence.

- Refer to List 49, Giving Directions, for other demonstration talks.

B. MINI-TALKS

OBJECTIVE

To develop the student's ability to talk about a subject using good voice projection, inflections, eye contact and continuity.

APPLICATIONS

- Encourage students to use good eye contact, voice inflection and descriptive language to make their subjects interesting.

- Use a time limit appropriate to the age and experience of the students.

- Allow the student to give his speech before a small group of students rather than before a large class.

- Video tape and play back if possible.

List 91: Demonstration Talks

1. How to dissect a frog.
2. How to make icing and decorate a cake.
3. How to play Monopoly.
4. How to load a camera and take a picture.
5. How to ride a horse.
6. How to change and fix a bike tire.
7. How to play hopscotch.
8. How to make and fly a kite.
9. How to build a robot.
10. How to wash a car.

11. How to build a birdhouse.
12. How to play tetherball.
13. How to give a dog a bath.
14. How to wrap a present.
15. How to make a jack-o-lantern.
16. How to play a game of cards.
17. How to put on clown makeup.
18. How to play baseball.
19. How to decorate a Christmas tree.
20. How to make your favorite sandwich.
21. How to ice skate or roller skate.
22. How to make a puppet.
23. How a telephone works.
24. How to color eggs.
25. How to clean your room.
26. How to play checkers.
27. How to swim.
28. How to draw a dog.
29. How to ride a bike.
30. How to save someone who can't swim.
31. How to do a magic trick.
32. How to build a campfire.
33. How to plant a garden.
34. How to bowl.
35. How to make a paper airplane.

List 92: Mini-Talks

1. Tell a ghost story.
2. Tell your life history.
3. Tell the plot of your favorite movie.
4. Tell about the best birthday you ever had.
5. Tell about the State Fair or a carnival you have been to.
6. Tell what you would do with a million dollars.
7. Tell about the craziest thing that ever happened to you.
8. Tell about a time you got lost.
9. Tell about the craziest dream you ever had.
10. Tell about the best vacation you ever had.
11. Tell what you would do if you got lost in the desert.
12. Describe the neatest park you have ever seen.
13. Describe the scariest ride you have been on at an amusement park.
14. Tell all you know about sea monsters.
15. Tell all you know about Disneyland.
16. Tell all you know about growing vegetable gardens.
17. Tell all you know about ghosts.
18. Tell all you know about making movies.
19. Tell all you know about dinosaurs.
20. Tell how a car works.
21. Tell how a television works.
22. Tell all you know about the Civil War.
23. Tell all you know about sharks.
24. Tell all you know about werewolves.
25. Tell how a cartoon is made (animated).

List 93: People Talks

OBJECTIVE

To develop the student's ability to speak effectively before a group using an outline and notes.

APPLICATIONS

- It is important to give a demonstration talk first as a model for the students. Emphasize the *purpose* of the talk (introduction, biography, etc.). Also assist students with preparation of an outline or notes to follow.

- Stress vocal variety and projection.

- Refer to Lists 97 and 99 for names of other people to talk about. Also use people from literature, social studies and science in the curriculum as subjects.

Introduce (tell interesting details about their lives)

1. one of your parents
2. a state congressman
3. Napoleon
4. Abraham Lincoln
5. John F. Kennedy
6. Leonardo da Vinci
7. Betsy Ross
8. Snoopy
9. Helen Keller
10. Little Miss Muffet

Make a nominating speech for President about (give qualifications and accomplishments)

1. Charlie Chaplin
2. Walt Disney
3. Shirley Temple
4. your teacher
5. Robin Hood
6. Neil Armstrong
7. Old Mother Hubbard
8. Big Bird
9. Mr. Rogers
10. one of your friends

People Talks (continued)

Give a short biography of

1. Don Quixote
2. Daniel Boone
3. Elvis Presley
4. Howard Hughes
5. your grandfather
6. King Henry VIII
7. Sleeping Beauty
8. Pinocchio
9. your favorite sports hero
10. the President of the United States
11. your favorite singer or television star
12. the principal of your school
13. Martin Luther King
14. Abraham Lincoln
15. Madame Curie
16. Shirley Temple
17. Walt Disney
18. Thomas Edison
19. Charles Lindbergh
20. Luther Burbank

List 94: Commercials and Announcements

OBJECTIVE

To develop the student's ability to use creative and colorful language in describing an event or product.

APPLICATIONS

- **Commercials**
  Have the students listen to commercials. Discuss sales techniques used. Prepare a chart with these cues for giving commercials:

  Introduction
  Product name
  Special features
  Why you should buy it
  Where it is available
  Cost
  Ending

- Students should bring in a simulated product, props for demonstrations, or drawings to show. Encourage *specific* language in giving the talks.

- Talk about TV and radio terms such as timing, wind-up, cue cards, cut, sign-off, etc. Video-tape student commercials if possible for playback and discussion. Invite the parents in to watch them.

- **On-The-Spot Radio Announcements**
  Prepare a cue chart with WHO, WHERE, WHEN, and WHAT HAPPENED on it. Encourage the students to use vocal variety to make the talk lively and to use many descriptive adjectives.

- Refer to List 98, Historical Events, for other events to report.

- **Pet Parade**
  Have each student bring or select a stuffed animal. Have him describe it and tell interesting facts about it for a television show.

Give a TV commercial for:

1. a fantastic new glue

2. multi-vitamin bubble gum (a whole meal)

3. bicycle that converts to a boat

4. small flying saucer for kids

5. cloth that makes you invisible

6. detective kit

7. a puppy that never grows older

8. a robot that cleans your room

9. super jumping shoes
10. breakfast cereal that makes you super smart
11. disguise kit for all occasions
12. fishing pole guaranteed to catch fish
13. electric baseball bat
14. a picture telephone
15. your own invention
16. any real product

Give an on-the-spot exciting radio announcement about:

1. a UFO is sighted above the city
2. millions of grasshoppers are coming over the city
3. a Little League player hit a ball one mile
4. a lady millionaire is giving away silver dollars at the library
5. a computer has gone crazy
6. the bones of a dinosaur have been discovered in the city park
7. a 2-year-old baby has saved a man's life
8. Martians have landed in Los Angeles
9. dogs and cats have learned to talk
10. a motorcyclist is going to jump the Grand Canyon
11. the filming of a Presidential news conference
12. how it feels to be parachuting from an airplane unexpectedly
13. a deep sea diver has just found a city under water

List 95: Interview Topics

OBJECTIVE

To develop the student's ability to interact verbally with another student with clarity of thought and speech and to ask pertinent questions.

APPLICATIONS

♦ Prepare a chart to assist the interviewer. Include the following:

WHO   WHERE   WHEN   WHAT   WHY

♦ Have students watch a "talk show" on television to get ideas for questioning techniques.

♦ Encourage the person being interviewed to assume the total character of the famous person. Consider the age, speech pattern, posture and personality.

♦ Have the interviewer hold a microphone or facsimile. Record or video tape the interview for evaluation later. This is also good for building self–concept.

♦ Refer to Lists 97 and 99 for names of others to be interviewed and to List 98 for related historical events.

1. Babe Ruth about his baseball career
2. a character from a book you are reading
3. Nadia Comaneche or Bruce Jenner on training for Olympics
4. the Troll under the Three Billy Goats' bridge
5. Martin Luther King on his struggle for civil rights
6. Adam and Eve in the Garden of Eden
7. Wright Brothers with their first airplane
8. President of the United States about nuclear wars
9. the first doctor to do a heart transplant
10. Santa Claus on the night before Christmas
11. Jack (of the Beanstalk) and his adventure
12. Muhammad Ali before one of his big fights
13. Charlie Bucket after he won the Chocolate Factory
14. Little Miss Muffet after she ran away
15. Cinderella at midnight
16. Robinson Crusoe after he was found on the island
17. Ben Franklin about his kite experiment
18. Lincoln about freeing the slaves
19. the Beatles about making records and their climb to success
20. Noah before he set sail on the Ark

21. Alexander Bell on how his telephone works
22. Queen Elizabeth on what she does on a typical day
23. Florence Nightingale about first aid during the war.
24. Heidi on the advantages of mountain living
25. Groucho Marx on the life of a comedian
26. Chris Evert on tennis tips for young players
27. Goldilocks on what a bear's house is like
28. the Governor of your state on his responsibilities
29. the person who invented the mirror
30. the person who accidentally discovered popcorn

List 96: Improvisations

OBJECTIVE

To develop the student's ability to improvise a story and act it out with other students using verbal and non-verbal language.

APPLICATIONS

♦ These scenes are to be used after students have worked on body language and storytelling (see Lists 81 through 86 and List 90). Talk about being *believable* and staying in character in improvisation.

♦ Give students a scene plan and allow a few minutes for them to plan the location and sequence of the scene. They may wish to use a few simple props or hats.

♦ Discuss the scene afterwards. "I could really believe they were by a campfire. Bill looked so cold." "I liked the way Jean got in and out of the car." "What did you like about their scene?"

♦ Let two more students repeat the same scene and improve upon it or change it.

♦ Use scenes from material you are studying currently (literature, social studies, science, etc.) or from stories students have written.

♦ Refer to Lists 97 and 98 for other ideas for scenes. The Story Openers, List 90, may also be used for improvisations.

♦ Tell a story (see Lists 99 and 100) to the students. Discuss the characters — how they walk, talk, feel, etc. Let the students choose roles and act out the story. You can narrate or take one of the roles to keep the action going.

1. You are in an elevator.
   It stops between floors and you cannot get the door open.
   Discuss what to do.
   What happens?

2. You are out camping.
   It gets very cold even though you are in sleeping bags.
   Decide what to do.

3. You are at a used car lot.
   The salesman shows you a car and gives a sales pitch.
   You try to get it cheaper.

4. You want a raise in pay.
   You nervously approach your employer and explain.
   He doesn't want to give you one.

5. You are scientists working on a potion.
   One of you accidentally spills it on the other one and something strange happens.

6. You are on the desert and need water badly.
   Keep looking.
   Finally one of you finds a stream.

7. You are paddling a canoe.
   Discover a leak.
   It keeps getting bigger and you try to save the canoe.
   Show what happens.

8. Come home from school and you are locked out.
   Try and find a way to get into the house.
   What do you do?

9. Walk up to a haunted house.
   Open the door and go in carefully.
   Show what you hear and see.
   What happens?

10. You are in a tennis tournament.
    You lose the final match and your best friend tries to make you feel better.

11. Argue with your sister or brother on whose turn it is to do the dishes.
    How will you work it out?

12. You build a robot.
    To your surprise, he works.
    He follows your commands.

13. You are in a foreign country and get lost.
    No one speaks English.
    Show how you communicate with someone trying to help you.

14. You are playing baseball.
    You disagree with the umpire's call.
    Show what happens.

15. You are driving a car fast.
    A policeman stops to give you a ticket.
    You try to talk him out of it.

16. A nurse must give a little child a shot.
    He is very scared.
    Show what they do.

17. A salesman comes to your home selling vacuum cleaners.
    You don't want any but he is determined to sell you one.

18. You are a paper carrier and you accidentally toss a paper through a window.
    The owner comes out mad.
    Show what happens.

19. You go to a restaurant and order your dinner from the waiter.
    When he comes, he spills soup all over you.
    Show what happens.

20. You take your little sister to the circus.
    Watch the clowns, the high wire walker, the trapeze artists, and the animals.
    Buy hot dogs and cotton candy.
    Your sister gets tired.
    You have to take her home.

VI. Helpful Lists (to be used with other lists)

97. Famous people

98. Historical events

99. Fictional characters

100. Other stories for improvisations

List 97: Famous People

Inventions — Discoveries
Louis Pasteur (pasteurizing process)
Alexander Graham Bell (telephone)
Thomas Edison (electric light)
Madame Curie (radium)
Albert Einstein (theory of relativity)
Benjamin Franklin (printing press)
Orville and Wilbur Wright (airplane)
Robert Fulton (steamboat)
Cavemen (wheel and fire)
Henry Ford (automobile)
Eli Whitney (cotton gin)
Galileo (telescope)
Isaac Newton (gravity)
Jonas Salk (polio vaccine)
Guglielmo Marconi (telegraph)

Sports
Olga Korbut
Nadia Comaneche
Muhammed Ali
Bruce Jenner
Babe Ruth
Mark Spitz
Billie Jean King
Jim Thorpe
Péle
Hank Aaron
Dorothy Hamil
Chris Evert
Joe Louis

Historical
John Hancock
Abraham Lincoln
George Washington
Paul Revere
Betsy Ross
Christopher Columbus
King Henry VIII
Winston Churchill
Queen Elizabeth
Julius Caesar
Napoleon Bonaparte
George Washington Carver
Presidents of the U.S.
Martin Luther King
Theodore Roosevelt

Cesar Chavez
Patrick Henry
Aristotle
Harriet Tubman
Florence Nightingale
King Tutankhamen
Pocahontas
Buffalo Bill
General Custer
Daniel Boone
Amelia Earhardt
Davy Crockett

Biblical
David and Goliath
Noah
Moses
Daniel in the Lion's Den
Adam and Eve

Entertainment
W. C. Fields
Elvis Presley
Roy Rogers
Groucho Marx
Abbott and Costello
Charlie Chaplin
Shirley Temple
Walt Disney
Charles Schultz (Peanuts)
Edward Villella (ballet)
The Beatles

Artists, Writers and Composers
Francis Scott Key
Mark Twain
Ernest Hemingway
Beethoven
William Shakespeare
Agatha Christie
Will Rogers
Charles Dickens
Edgar Allen Poe
Jack London
Hans Christian Anderson
Leonardo da Vinci
Michelangelo
Picasso

List 98: Historical Events

These may be used for improvisations, on-the-spot reports, interviews or story-telling.

1. Cavemen invent the wheel
2. Building of pyramids in Egypt
3. Stone Age men tame the first animal
4. Discovery of fire
5. Noah and the Great Flood
6. Eruption of Mt. Vesuvius
7. Murder of Julius Caesar
8. First Olympic Games
9. Crowning of Charlemagne (Christmas 800 AD)
10. Invention of the printing press
11. Invention of gunpowder and fireworks in China
12. King Arthur creates the Knights of the Round Table
13. Leif Erickson discovers the New World
14. Travels of Marco Polo
15. Christopher Columbus meets with King Ferdinand and Queen Isabella and sets sail
16. Ponce de Leon looks for the Fountain of Youth in Florida
17. Pilgrims land at Plymouth Rock
18. The First Thanksgiving
19. Boston Tea Party
20. Midnight ride of Paul Revere
21. Washington crossing the Delaware
22. Betsy Ross makes the first flag
23. Signing of the Declaration of Independence
24. Life on the Frontier
25. Invention of the first hot-air balloon
26. Lewis and Clark expedition
27. The meeting of the first railroads in the U.S. (sinking of the golden spike)
28. Invention of the telegraph
29. Jesse James robs the train
30. Scenes from young Abe Lincoln's life
31. Surrender of General Lee to General Grant
32. Abolition of slavery
33. Invention of the telephone

34. Invention of the first motor car

35. Wright Brothers invent the airplane

36. Edison records on the phonograph (Mary Had a Little Lamb)

37. Invention of the first silent movies

38. Discovery of the Tomb of King Tut

39. Sinking of the Titanic

40. First television set

41. John Glenn orbits the earth

42. First men set foot on the moon

43. Hank Aaron makes all-time career home run record

44. Bruce Jenner wins the Decathlon in the Olympics

List 99: Fictional Characters

Nursery Rhymes
- Little Miss Muffet
- Georgie Porgie
- Jack Horner
- Jack Sprat
- Humpty Dumpty
- Little Bo Peep
- Tommy Tucker
- Mistress Mary
- Old King Cole
- Simple Simon
- Solomon Grundy
- Queen of Hearts
- Tom, the Piper's Son
- Old Mother Hubbard
- Little Boy Blue
- Wee Willie Winkie
- Three Little Kittens
- Peter the Pumpkin Eater
- Old Woman in the Shoe
- Jack and Jill
- Owl and the Pussycat

Fiction
- Cinderella
- Peter Rabbit
- Rumplestiltskin
- Snow White
- Sleeping Beauty
- Hansel and Gretel
- Pied Piper

- Red Riding Hood
- Chicken Little
- Henny Penny
- Gingerbread Man
- Goldilocks
- The Three Bears
- Tom Thumb
- Rapunzel
- Alice in Wonderland
- Mother Goose
- King Midas
- Troll in 3 Billy Goats Gruff
- Big Bad Wolf
- The Three Pigs
- Wizard of Oz
- Winnie the Pooh
- Brer Rabbit
- Peter Pan
- Ferdinand the Bull
- Aladdin
- Pinocchio
- Raggedy Ann and Andy
- Mary Poppins
- Peter Piper
- Heidi
- Dumbo
- Bambi
- Rip Van Winkle
- Robin Hood
- Scrooge
- Robinson Crusoe
- Frankenstein
- Tom Sawyer
- Huckleberry Finn
- King Arthur
- Sir Lancelot
- Guinevere
- Sinbad
- William Tell
- Johnnie Appleseed
- Captain Hook
- Ichabod Crane
- Headless Horseman
- Tarzan
- Dracula
- Moby Dick
- Romeo and Juliet
- Paul Bunyan
- Sherlock Holmes
- Dr. Jekyll and Mr. Hyde
- Don Quixote

Tiny Tim
Yankee Doodle
Willie Wonka
Charlie (of the Chocolate Factory)
Cat in the Hat

Other

Snoopy
Charlie Brown
Lucy
Spiderman
Superman
King Kong
Mickey Mouse
Minnie Mouse

Bugs Bunny
Big Bird
Santa Claus
Easter Bunny
Dennis the Menace
Popeye
Pink Panther
Fred Flintstone
Donald Duck
Dumbo
Yogi Bear
Batman and Robin
Wonder Woman
Mr. Magoo
Lassie

List 100: Other Stories for Improvisation

1. The Tortoise and the Hare (La Fontaine)
2. The Lion and the Mouse (Aesop)
3. Stone in the Road (traditional)
4. The Shepherd Boy and the Wolf (Aesop)
5. The Elves and the Shoemaker (Grimm)
6. Little Red Hen (traditional)
7. Musicians of Bremen (Grimm)
8. Caps for Sale (Esther Slobodkin)
9. The Princess Who Could Not Cry (Rose Fyleman)
10. Town Mouse and Country Mouse (Aesop)
11. The Emperor's New Clothes (Hans Christian Andersen)
12. Where the Wild Things Are (Maurice Sendak)
13. The Sneetches (Dr. Seuss)
14. The Princess on the Pea (Hans Christian Andersen)
15. Winnie the Pooh Goes Visiting (A. A. Milne)
16. Scenes from Willie Wonka and the Chocolate Factory (Roald Dahl)
17. Rip Van Winkle (Washington Irving)
18. Horton Hatches the Egg (Dr. Seuss)
19. Are You My Mother? (Paul Galdone)
20. The Grinch Who Stole Christmas (Dr. Seuss)
21. A Christmas Carol (Charles Dickens)
22. The Giving Tree (Shel Silverstein)
23. Brer Rabbit and His Tricks (Ennis Rees)
24. Just So Stories (Rudyard Kipling)
25. Greek Myths (see Olivia Coolidge)

26. Once on a Mouse (Marcia Brown)
27. Stone Soup (Marcia Brown)
28. Scenes from Alice in Wonderland (Lewis Carroll)
29. Scenes from the Wizard of Oz (Ed Emberley)
30. Our Lady's Juggler (Legend)
31. The Bishop's Candlesticks (Victor Hugo)
32. Andy and the Lion (James Dougherty)
33. The Story of Ferdinand (Munro Leaf)
34. Harry, The Dirty Dog (Gene Zion)
35. Mr. Rabbit and The Lovely Present (Maurice Sendak)
36. The Squire's Bride (Gudrun Thorne-Thomsen)
37. The Fir Tree (Hans Christian Andersen)
38. The Tinderbox (Hans Christian Andersen)
39. Abe Lincoln's Other Mother (Bernadine Bailey)
40. Ask Mr. Bear (Marjorie Flack)

NOTE: See also List 99, Fictional Characters, for other story suggestions.

Appendix

Appendix

PATTERNS FOR STUDENTS' STORIES

1. On the following pages are patterns which may be used for recording children's own stories. The shapes may be cut out of construction paper. Use several colors for variety. Print the stories with fine-line colored markers.

2. Select a subject to stimulate ideas and create a mood. This can be one from current class curriculum or from current events or interest (i.e., occupations, travel, circus, sports, etc.). Play a related record, show pictures or slides of related objects, act out a story or role-play, introduce new vocabulary and concepts on the subject and share experiences.

3. Have each child dictate a story about the subject. Print it on the shape. You may wish to help the child by asking such questions as: "What happened next?", "Did something exciting happen then?", "What did he do then?".

4. Read the stories to the children, using lots of expression and excitement in your voice. Encourage the classroom teacher and parents to read the stories aloud for further reinforcement.

5. Hang the stories up for other children to read and finally send them home to be hung up and enjoyed by the families. Encourage parents to save all the stories in a folder for the child to read at the end of the year.

6. The students may also wish to decorate or draw on the other side of the shape story.

7. You might arrange to display your young authors' stories in the library. Children really enjoy reading the stories of other students.

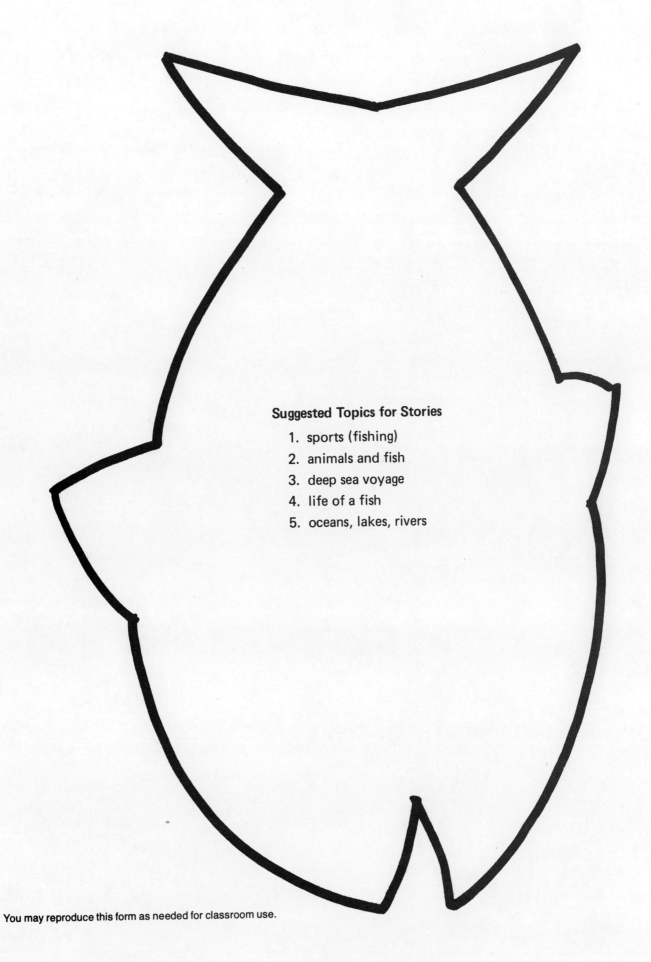

Suggested Topics for Stories

1. sports (fishing)
2. animals and fish
3. deep sea voyage
4. life of a fish
5. oceans, lakes, rivers

You may reproduce this form as needed for classroom use.

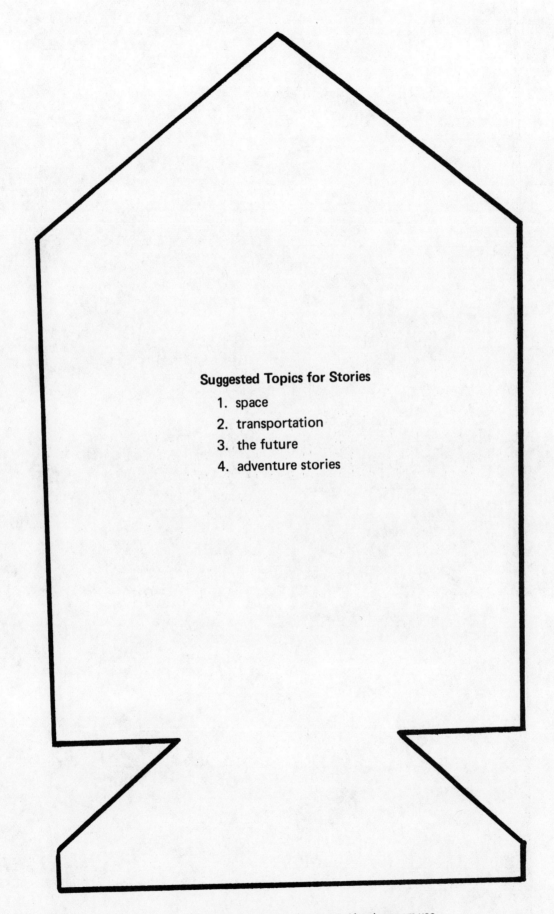

Suggested Topics for Stories

1. space
2. transportation
3. the future
4. adventure stories

Suggested Topics for Stories

1. circus
2. occupations
3. if I were a clown
4. magic tricks

You may reproduce this form as needed for classroom use.

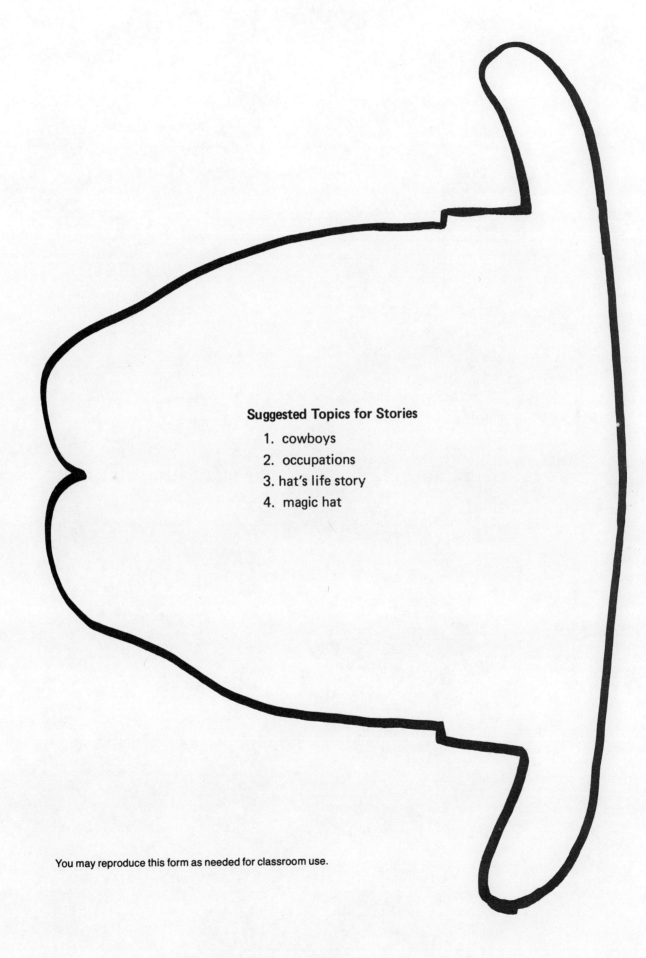

Suggested Topics for Stories

1. cowboys
2. occupations
3. hat's life story
4. magic hat

You may reproduce this form as needed for classroom use.

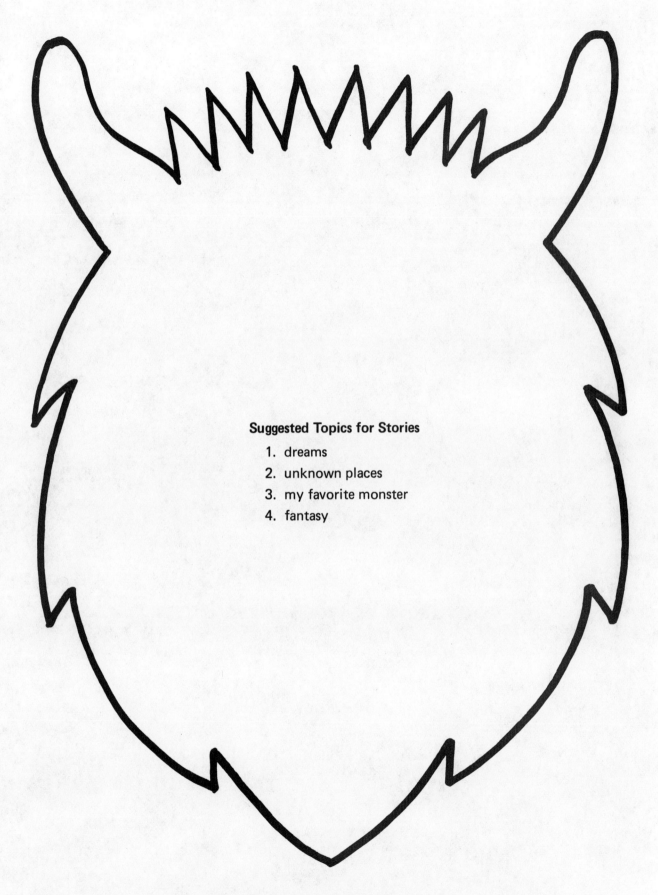

Suggested Topics for Stories

1. dreams
2. unknown places
3. my favorite monster
4. fantasy

You may reproduce this form as needed for classroom use.

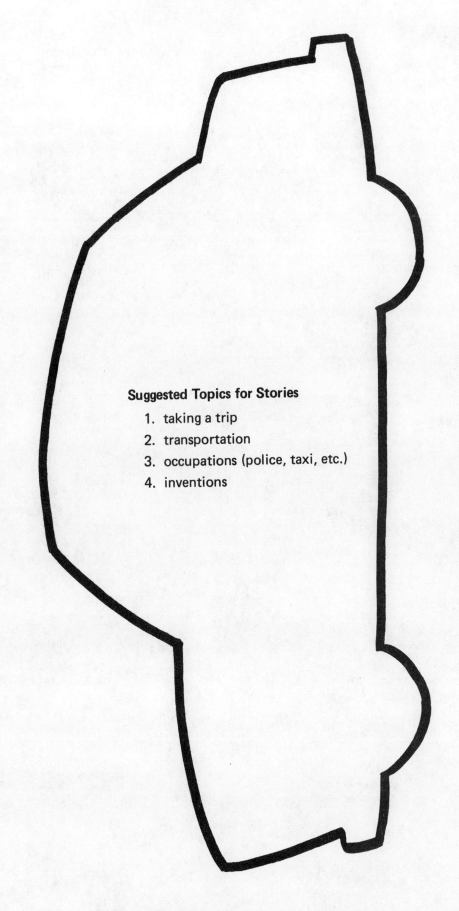

Suggested Topics for Stories

1. taking a trip
2. transportation
3. occupations (police, taxi, etc.)
4. inventions

Skills Index

The following list groupings may be helpful in teaching individual skills.

Analyzing — 22, 28–30, 35, 40, 50–51, 52–80, 91–96

Articulation Carryover — 36–40, 69–75, 88–96

Classifying — 63–68, 82–86

Closure, prediction and using context clues — 2, 23–27, 43–46, 52–62, 76–79, 88

Constructing and expanding sentences — 17, 88–96

Creating language — 1, 17, 33, 81–96

Following directions and memory — 20, 47–49, 87, 96

Listening, observing and interpreting — 20, 33, 49, 81–87, 96

Manual expression — 21, 23–30, 33, 40, 42, 81–87, 96, 100

Rhyming — 1, 2, 50–51, 77

Sequencing — 15–16 (words), 41–42 (sentences), 47–49 (directions), 80 (logical sequence), 87, 91, 96 (actions). See also *Sound Blending and Syllabication.*

Sound Blending — 7, 8, 9, 10

Structural analysis — 3–6, 11–14, 18, 21

Syllabication — 3, 4, 5, 6

Verbal Expression — Most of the lists can be used for verbal expression as oral responses are encouraged in each task.

Vocabulary expansion — 13–14, 19, 21–33, 50–51, 65–68